Library of
Davidson College

POLITICAL CHANGE IN BAJA CALIFORNIA

MONOGRAPH SERIES, 40
CENTER FOR U.S.-MEXICAN STUDIES
UNIVERSITY OF CALIFORNIA, SAN DIEGO

POLITICAL CHANGE IN BAJA CALIFORNIA

DEMOCRACY IN THE MAKING?

VICTORIA E. RODRÍGUEZ
AND
PETER M. WARD

Center for U.S.-Mexican Studies
University of California, San Diego

THE CENTER FOR U.S.-MEXICAN STUDIES
UNIVERSITY OF CALIFORNIA, SAN DIEGO

All rights reserved. Published 1994

Printed in the United States of America

Cover photograph: Architects of Democracy—Carlos Salinas de Gortari, President of Mexico, and Ernesto Ruffo Appel, Governor of Baja California

Cover design by Blaize, Publications Department, UCSD

ISBN 1-878367-25-0

Contents

List of Tables and Figures	vi
A Note on Authorship	vii
Acknowledgments	viii
Introduction—Mexico's Political System—A "Perfect Dictatorship" or an "Imperfect Democracy"?	1
Chapter 1—Democratization at Mexico's Center and in the Periphery	9
Chapter 2—Democratization through *Alternancia* and the Changing Electoral Process	29
Chapter 3—Political Recruitment, Government, and Partisanship	53
Chapter 4—Intragovernmental Relations: The Separation of Powers	81
Chapter 5—Democratization through Decentralization: The Changing Nature of Intergovernmental Relations	99
Chapter 6—Architects of Democracy? Changing Political Traditions in Mexico	119
Acronyms	129
References	131
About the Authors	139

Tables and Figures

Tables

1.1	Population Growth by State, Municipality, and Principal Urban Center, 1960–1990	20
1.2	Rural and Urban Population by Municipality, 1960–1990	20
1.3	Service Deficits for Dwellings in Baja California by Municipality, 1970–1990	21
1.4	Rate of GDP Growth by Sector, 1940–1980	23
1.5	Broad Industrial Subsectors by Municipality, 1984	24
1.6	Economically Active Population by Sector and Municipality, 1980	25
2.1	Gubernatorial Election Results for Baja California since 1953	40
2.2	PRI and PAN Vote in Municipal Elections, 1986–1992	41
2.3	Votes by Party in State Congressional Elections, 1986–1992	42

Figures

5.1	Baja California's Self-generated Revenues, 1988–1991	108
5.2	Tax Revenues Registered in Mexicali and Tijuana during the 1980s	113
5.3	Principal Revenue Sources for Tijuana, Mexicali, and Ensenada, 1990 and 1991	114

A Note on Authorship

In the acknowledgments to this volume we record our gratitude and appreciation to the Policy Research Project graduate students who worked with us during 1992 and 1993. Although the current text is largely our own, these students participated fully in the fieldwork and analysis, and in the preparation of some of the original chapter drafts. Therefore, we should like to recognize the following individuals as part-authors of this book:

- Steven Andrew Barracca
- Matthew James Burns, III
- Ramiro Canales
- Beth Hilary Cohen
- Serge Dedina
- Roger Douglas Frahm
- Dominic F. Giarrantani
- Petra Lanz
- Shannan L. Mattiace
- Elizabeth Hope Morrison
- Robert James O'Donnell
- Jorge G. Reyes-Escatel
- Margarita Treviño Ballí
- Joanne V. Ureña

Naturally, we remain responsible for any errors of fact or of interpretation which may remain.

Acknowledgments

We were extremely fortunate when conducting the research reported in this volume to have the support of an enthusiastic group of students, who also proved to be extremely capable researchers. Working together was a true pleasure. Many of our insights came out of class discussions, and particularly from our impassioned debates about whether the glass of democracy was half full or half empty.

Funding for this round of research was provided by the Hewlett Foundation through its grant to the U.S.-Mexican Policy Studies Program at the Lyndon B. Johnson School of Public Affairs, University of Texas at Austin. We are grateful for the support that Professor Sidney Weintraub, director of the program, gave to our research. We should also like to express our gratitude to the LBJ School's dean, Max Sherman, and to the director of the Institute of Latin American Studies at UT, Professor Peter Cleaves, both of whom, at different stages, provided us with generous support. We wish to thank Professor Wayne Cornelius for inviting us to present our preliminary findings at the Center for U.S.-Mexican Studies at the University of California, San Diego, and subsequently to submit this monograph for inclusion in the Center's publications series.

We also wish to thank two anonymous referees whose careful review of the manuscript and detailed suggestions were extremely helpful in guiding some of the final revisions, particularly in light of the events unfolding in Mexico since the fall of 1993 and the run-up to the August 1994 elections. Likewise, we are grateful to Kevin Middlebrook of the Center for U.S.-Mexican Studies at UCSD for his detailed comments and suggestions.

On behalf of the research team, we must thank all of those in Baja California who gave of their time to talk with us. We hope that the arguments expressed in this volume will reflect positively upon their endeavors to construct a democracy "without adjectives" in their state. The people of Baja California, regardless of their individual party affiliations, are to be congratulated: whether or not they will be successful in the long term remains to be seen, but at this moment they are in the vanguard of democratization in Mexico and are giving it their best shot. This book is about their best shot.

Introduction

Mexico's Political System—A "Perfect Dictatorship" or an "Imperfect Democracy"?

For many years Mexico's political system has attracted attention and been widely admired, largely because of its stability in a continent renowned for coups, countercoups, and authoritarian governments. The two descriptions alluded to in the above title come from internationally known contemporary novelists. The first, the "perfect dictatorship," was coined by Peruvian Mario Vargas Llosa soon after Carlos Salinas de Gortari was elected to the Mexican presidency in 1988. The second, the "imperfect democracy," is the description offered by Mexican author Carlos Fuentes. Significantly, the former, more critical description (offered by an outsider to the Mexican context) reflects the grudging admiration that many Latin Americans hold for Mexico's disguised authoritarian structure. Equally significant is that the second and more forgiving description should come from a Mexican intellectual who, like many of his compatriots, is often critical of the Mexican political system and its shortcomings, yet also appreciates the important strides that it is making toward becoming a more genuine democracy. Although we, too, are outsiders, our view concurs with that of Fuentes: Mexico remains an imperfect democracy. The question is, of course, how imperfect. Is it becoming more or less democratic? Certainly, on the surface at least, there have been important reforms to the electoral process, some of them last-minute changes undertaken just two months before the August 21, 1994, presidential election. Perhaps the most important of these was the change in the composition of the General Council of the Federal Electoral Institute—the maximum electoral authority—which oversaw the conduct of the elections and the calculation and declaration of the results. These changes are discussed in further detail below.

As was always anticipated, the August 21, 1994, elections proved to be an acid test of how far Mexico had come in the democratization of its electoral procedures. Although there were significant "irregularities" in a substantial number of voting precincts, the general consensus appears to have been that the elections represented a major advance in the way in which elections are conducted in Mexico.[1] In short, the elections were considered to be relatively clean, but not fair. The unfairness relates to the uneven electoral playing field that persists in Mexico, systematically favoring the dominant Institutional Revolutionary Party (PRI)—principally through privileged access to and influence over the media, the enormous advantages this party enjoys in campaign financing (despite limits imposed in 1993), and the direct association of federal government programs such as PRONASOL with the governing party. Some observers see this stacking of the deck to the PRI's advantage as the crucial determinant of President Ernesto Zedillo's and the PRI's success in the August 1994 elections. These unfair advantages are increasingly seen as constituting an important medium of fraud, and there seems little doubt that all three areas will be subject to review and reform as part of President Zedillo's inauguration promise to make the 1997 elections clean, fair, and credible.

The research upon which we report in this monograph forms part of a wider project entitled "Politics, Power, and Public Administration in Urban Mexico: The Experience and Future of Opposition Parties in Government." When we began the research in 1989, it was especially timely, as many countries in Latin America had emerged from long periods of dictatorship and bureaucratic authoritarian regimes. Countries such as Brazil, Argentina, and Chile were struggling to find a stable path through the pluralistic political environment that they had recently created. Outside the continent, China and the former Soviet Union were also undertaking major economic restructuring, moving from command economies to more mixed arrangements and opening up their political systems. The Chinese experiment was very quickly nipped in the bud, but the collapse of the Soviet system and the subsequent democratization of Eastern Europe heightened interest in these processes worldwide. These countries, invariably starting from scratch, began to create structures with reduced state intervention, market economies, voting and pluralism, new leaders and new cadres of bureaucrats, new social organizations, and often whole new political cultures. These were exciting times indeed, particularly because often the old guard was not completely swept away. As a result, these experiments very quickly ran into entrenched resistance which slowed the transition toward democracy. Sometimes, too, there were countercoups, although thus far none of these has proven to be ultimately successful.

---

[1] Foweraker (in Ward et al. 1994: 43) suggests that Mexico now has democratic elections but without democracy. See also Gómez Tagle and Garrido in Ward et al. 1994 (pages 38–39 and 73–75, respectively).

In Mexico, also, the changes have been dramatic. But interestingly, the country no longer represents the vanguard of democratization within Latin America, since many countries have overtaken it in their political opening. The fragile facade of democracy has no longer been sufficient to legitimize successive governments of Mexico's ruling Institutional Revolutionary Party. After the contentious presidential elections of 1988, president-elect Salinas declared the end of what had in effect been a one-party system. For the first time, non-PRI senators gained election to Congress, and in 1989 Baja California became the first state in the history of contemporary Mexico to be governed by a party other than the PRI. In an electoral outcome that stunned many observers, Ernesto Ruffo Appel, of the National Action Party (PAN), became governor of that state. An assessment of his government, coupled with an analysis of the relations between the federal PRIísta center and the opposition in the periphery, is the subject of this book.

Research Framework

As noted earlier, the material contained in this volume represents the second stage of a wider research project on Mexico's governments of the opposition. The overall project has five principal research objectives. First, it aims to assess the effectiveness and capacity of opposition parties in Mexico to respond to the challenges of exercising power. Second, it proposes to analyze the extent to which partisan political rationality intervenes in the calculus of urban and statewide administration and decision making. Third, it seeks to examine intergovernmental relations among the federal, state, and municipal levels, focusing in particular upon relations between governments of different political parties. Fourth, it intends to assess the validity and viability of contemporary democratization processes in Mexico—asking, in short, how genuine was the political opening of the 1980s and what factors are most likely to determine the success or failure of that process during the 1990s. The fifth and final aim is to examine some of the implications of political pluralism for political and administrative decentralization. The issues of deconcentration, decentralization, and devolution remain firmly on the contemporary political agenda, but the extent to which any of these options is adopted relates closely to the emergence of pluralism and to the nature of intergovernmental relations.

In the first stage of this project we focused solely upon the 1983–1986 PANista municipal governments of Francisco Barrio and Luis H. Alvarez in Ciudad Juárez and Chihuahua, respectively (see Rodríguez and Ward 1992). The present study also considers municipal government experiences of both the PAN and the PRI, but within the wider context of the PAN's exercise of power at the state level in this, the first experience of opposition government in a Mexican state. The third phase of the research, not reported upon here directly, explored some municipal government experiences of the other principal opposition party in Mexico, the Party of the Democratic Revolution (PRD), in the state of Michoacán, as well as PANista experiences in Zamora, Michoacán, and San Pedro Garza García, Nuevo León. It also examined the ways in which the PRI has responded to these opposition initiatives. As our research has progressed we have become increasingly aware that the PRI is adopting strategies of urban governance that are more transparent, equitable, and efficient. Thus, in the case of the Monterrey metropolitan area we have investigated both PRIísta and PANista governments.[2]

Ultimately, the aim is to analyze the research questions outlined above across a wide range of experiences that will embrace old and new, big and small, and rich and poor state and municipal governments of the opposition. We hope this will allow us to produce a work that encompasses the rich diversity of Mexico's contemporary governments. We hope, too, that we will be able to assess whether the process of democratization is leading toward what Enrique Krauze (1986) has termed a democracy "without adjectives."

Methodology

All three phases of fieldwork for this research have been undertaken through the Lyndon B. Johnson School of Public Affairs at the University of Texas at Austin, in conjunction with graduate student assistance from and participation of the School, the Government Department, and the Institute of Latin American Studies. Our research has relied heavily upon the energetic participation and commitment of the students who took our year-long Policy Research Project seminar during the 1992–1993 academic session. The seminar developed through a series of stages. The first provided the students with an intensive introduction to the nature of the Mexican political system, after which we began to draw up a contextual background of our case study area, identifying principal issues of conflict and the key actors and groups involved. The first trawl was provided by a systematic archival analysis of two magazines: *Proceso*, which covers Mexican national politics in a fairly objective though critical manner; and *La Nación*, which is the official publication of the PAN. Based upon this

---

[2]This has resulted in the production of three internal "working papers" which are available for consultation upon application to the authors. They are: "The New PRI: Recasting Its Identity"; "From Machine Politics to the Politics of Technocracy"; and "The PRD in Power: Missed Opportunities in the Spotlight."

contextual analysis conducted for the 1983–1986 period for Ensenada under the Socialist Workers' Party (PST)[3] and 1989–1993 for the state as a whole (including its four municipalities), we were able to draw up a framework and broad "Who's Who" for a content analysis of the newspapers in each city for specific periods. In the first round of fieldwork, our researchers went to three cities (Ensenada, Mexicali, and Tijuana), where they reviewed one or more of the following newspapers: *El Mexicano, La Voz de la Frontera, Diario 29,* and the weekly *Zeta*. In summary form this provided us with a detailed contextual analysis and chronology, covering the principal actors and issues engaged in urban politics and administration statewide and in each city, as well as a preliminary indication of the bases of support that existed for each party.

At the same time, the researchers collected data about each city and about the state in general in order to provide an overview of the political economy of Baja California. With these two contextual documents in mind, individual research agendas were drawn up for members of the research teams. The teams were organized to conduct fieldwork in either one of the three cities or in the state government. Unfortunately, this second round of fieldwork coincided with the torrential rains and disaster relief effort in Tijuana in early January 1993. This meant that teams were unable to gather much information at the neighborhood (*colonia*) level, but they were able to observe how city and state government responded to the crisis. The research agendas covered themes such as finances and intergovernmental relations, governmental structures and priorities, implementation of programs and public works, the rationality of decision making, government-neighborhood relations, political and electoral mobilization, and a detailed analysis of the workings of the state congress. In each case, research agendas were discussed and developed in order to ensure consistency between individuals working in different cities and to reduce any overlap that might otherwise have occurred within teams. In addition, in March 1993 we conducted a further set of interviews, including a meeting with Baja California Governor Ernesto Ruffo.

More than thirty past and present functionaries and politicians from both the PRI and the PAN were interviewed across a wide range of departments. Subsequently, these data, interview findings, and archival information were analyzed in depth and written up in four substantive documents which followed a common framework and which we called "base documents." These provided the foundation for

---

[3] Prior to Ruffo's victory as Ensenada's municipal president in 1986, the municipal president for Ensenada had been David Ojeda Ochoa, who won the municipality for the PST in 1983. However, the PST was a flag of convenience; Ojeda was a disaffected PRIísta who had unsuccessfully sought the local PRI nomination and then ran as a PST candidate.

systematic comparative discussions by the research teams and eventually became the basis for the following chapters.

Organizational Framework

This book examines Mexico's process of democratization in the periphery and the pattern of intergovernmental relations that emerged both locally and with the center, often cutting across party lines. Specifically, our aims are to examine the electoral successes of the PAN in Baja California, as well as to assess how the PANistas won power—or, as some would argue, how victory was conceded to them. Is this part of an evolution, or was it rather a Salinas construction to increase pluralism? Another aim is to examine how an opposition without experience forms governmental teams and goes about addressing issues of development and establishing an agenda for urban policy. Does such an opposition create new institutions, or does it adapt old ones? Similarly, in the implementation of policy, does it develop new bureaucratic routines or engage in partisan disbursement of resources? In short, what are the overall outcomes of government? A further aim is to analyze the links between governments and citizenry and to evaluate the creation of new opportunities for civic organization. Finally, how do newly emerging governments respond to the old guard, whether they be entrenched national and local political interests or militants within the governing party itself who have been excluded from the new regime?

In chapter 1 our purpose is to review the traditional political structure in Mexico and to introduce some of the major changes that have occurred since the mid-1970s. We also differentiate between the concepts of political and democratic transition before providing an introduction to the geography, economy, and society of our case study, Baja California. In chapters 2 through 5 we develop the substantive issues that have arisen from our fieldwork and research. Each of these four chapters seeks to tease out the extent to which democratization is occurring in Baja California. Chapter 2, for example, analyzes election results and changes in the wider electoral process in order to assess the prospects for ongoing pluralism and the alternation in power of different parties. Chapter 3 examines the structure of bureaucracy and government in Baja California—how they are staffed, how policy is implemented, and how relations with civic society change. Changes in the structure of political institutions and powers executive, legislative, and judicial are the focus of chapter 4. Here we evaluate the extent to which *intra*governmental changes are representative of, and conducive to, greater democratization at the local level. The patterns of *inter*governmental relations between different levels of political authority (state-federal, state-municipal, federal-municipal) and between different political parties are the subject of chapter 5. Here, too, we ask how far those relations are becoming more decentralized and to what extent local levels of government are experiencing increased autonomy and empowerment.

To anticipate our conclusions, we believe that democratization is occurring in a genuine way, albeit in forms that are often incipient and still fragile—but significant nevertheless. Our conclusions derive from three important processes which we use as "litmus test" indicators: (1) *alternancia* in power (i.e., competitive party politics leading to alternative parties acceding to government); (2) an active separation of powers (executive, legislative, and judicial), with checks and balances operating between them; and (3) decentralization and rising autonomy of local government. Each of these principal "tests" is analyzed in the substantive chapters that follow.

1

Democratization at Mexico's Center and in the Periphery

There are different interpretations of the nature of Mexico's democracy. Nevertheless, most analysts regard the Mexican political system as having some degree of authoritarianism. It is highly centralist, with enormous power vested in the presidency. The level of pluralism has been extremely limited, with only one party, the right-leaning National Action Party (PAN), offering any significant electoral opposition to the ruling Institutional Revolutionary Party (PRI). Even then, the share of the national vote officially conceded to the PAN has never been allowed to exceed 20 percent. Opposition parties on the left of the political spectrum have been either outlawed altogether or stage-managed by the PRI to provide some semblance of pluralism (González Casanova 1970). PRI presidential candidates have traditionally won 85 percent of the total vote, and PRI presidents ruled unchallenged in regular but nonrenewable six-year cycles (*sexenios*). Until 1979, elections were often rigged, both to prevent opposition parties from winning and to guarantee a level of support for the official party that was sufficient to legitimate the regime (Hansen 1974; Smith 1979; Camp 1993).[1] Such electoral rigging often was undertaken by local political machines seeking to curry favor at higher levels by demonstrating their capacity to "deliver" the vote.

Observers of Mexico also see traces of authoritarianism in the use of political repression and intimidation, which many believe to be

---

[1] There have also been occasions for suspecting the use of fraud to prevent opposition candidates from winning office. Many Mexicans believe that opposition candidates won the presidential elections of 1929, 1940, and 1988 (Camp 1993: 62). Others have argued that at various times in the recent past, opposition candidates were denied the governorships of San Luis Potosí, Chihuahua, and Baja California (see Bezdek 1995; Aziz Nassif 1987; Guillén López 1993). There are even more examples of municipal victories going unrecognized.

significant and systemic (Schers 1972; Bartra et al. 1975; Cockcroft 1983; Harvey 1989). Further, the press and other mass media are not immune to political pressures. By and large, the media follow the PRI line, and some journalists and publishers are known to have been on the government payroll (Riva Palacio 1993). Investigative journalists who dare to criticize the regime have been subject to intimidation, even assassination. Although the media have been relatively freer of government control since the mid-1970s, the norm throughout Mexico is still a compliant and PRI-supporting press.

This authoritarianism has not gone unchallenged. There have been periodic upwellings of dissent: student disturbances in 1968, rural guerrilla movements during the early 1970s, and the Chiapas insurrection in 1994. Mexico's labor unions have at times set themselves against the official, government-supported union structure; beginning in the 1970s several of these organizations broke away from their parent association to form more independent, democratic, and representative structures (Middlebrook 1991). Community organizations have challenged the state through coordinated urban social movements (Ramírez Saiz 1986; Foweraker and Craig 1990). Dissent was also manifest in the occasional municipal victory of an opposition party, but prior to the 1980s such an electoral upset was only likely to occur if popular dissatisfaction with the PRI or with a local power elite had become intense (Bezdek 1995).

During the 1960s, some senior leaders within the PRI, including party president Carlos Madrazo, aware of rising popular discontent, began advocating for internal democratic reform. By the beginning of the 1970s, the Mexican political system was in dire need of revitalization if it were to legitimize future PRI governments (González Casanova 1970).

Political versus Democratic Opening

The effort to revitalize and reform the political system began with a series of initiatives implemented in 1964; others followed in 1973 and 1977. Significantly, this process was referred to as *apertura política* (political opening), not *apertura democrática* (democratic opening). One important reform, instituted in 1973, allowed for the increased participation of a wide range of political parties, particularly from the left and including the Mexican Communist Party (PCM) after 1977. Perhaps the most important reform of all was the 1977 Federal Law of Political Organizations and Electoral Processes (LOPPE), which set aside one-fourth of the seats in the federal Chamber of Deputies to be divided among opposition parties proportionally, according to the percentage of the vote each received.[2] Although their legislative power remained highly constrained, opposition parties now had their foot in the door. The Chamber of Deputies was no longer blindly supportive of PRI- and executive-initiated legislation (Middlebrook 1986).

However, these reforms in no way lessened the authority or the role of the PRI government. Rather, they were intended to enhance and sustain it. Indeed, although the introduction of a deputy-at-large (*plurinominal*) system gave encouragement to opposition parties, their representation in the federal chamber between 1979 and 1985 remained roughly stable (Camp 1993: 148).

President Miguel de la Madrid (1982–1988) introduced a further reform in 1986 which was intended to extend opposition parties' opportunities for representation. Under this reform, the majority party may not hold more than 70 percent of the seats in the Chamber of Deputies. Further, it increased the number of total seats in both houses of Congress to five hundred, allocating three hundred to individuals elected by a plurality in their congressional districts, and two hundred to all registered parties, to be divided proportionally. This provision was further amended in 1987 to allow the party obtaining the greatest number of the three hundred majority seats to receive additional seats among those divided proportionally until it held an overall majority within Congress. The aim of this additional amendment, the so-called governability clause, was to ensure that the leading party could govern effectively, further constraining opposition parties' room for maneuver in Congress. (The governability clause was revoked in 1993.)

With these reforms in place, the 1988 elections proved to be historic. PRI presidential candidate Carlos Salinas de Gortari was elected with only 50 percent of the vote, the poorest showing in the party's history, and some claim that even this figure was achieved through fraud. Moreover, 1988 marks the first instance that opposition parties acquired a sufficient presence in the Chamber of Deputies to influence the policy-making and legislative processes (Mexican law requires a two-thirds majority vote to amend the constitution, and between 1988 and 1991 the PRI did not control two-thirds of deputy seats).

Despite gains made in the 1988 elections, Mexico's opposition parties were far from satisfied. In 1989 they began pressing for key constitutional amendments and for improvements in the conduct of electoral processes. The latter was achieved in 1990 when all parties in Congress except the Party of the Democratic Revolution (PRD) joined together to approve the Federal Code of Electoral Institutions and

---

[2] Although referred to in electoral law as proportional representation, it is not true proportional representation, which implies a division across the whole house.

Procedures (COFIPE), which paved the way for the creation of the Federal Electoral Institute (IFE).

Seeking additional reforms, opposition parties opened discussion on a number of issues, including the governability clause, political parties' uneven access to the media, the lack of controls on party and campaign financing, and the low level of pluralism in the Senate. However, congressional debate on these issues had reached a stalemate by 1993, and although the PRI could have easily built the necessary two-thirds majority to push through some innocuous reforms, it was reluctant to do so. In order to provide greater legitimacy for the 1994 elections, at minimum Salinas wanted PAN support for any reforms to the COFIPE. This meant that the reforms had to be approved by Congress before August 1993. The PRI offered several major last-minute concessions in order to win the PANistas' support, the most important of these being the PRI's promise to raise to four the number of senators from each state, one of whom was to be drawn from the party polling second best.[3] Other PRI concessions included greater equity in access to the media during campaigns; the imposition of limits on financial contributions to parties; the removal of the governability clause, which since 1987 had guaranteed the PRI a working majority in Congress;[4] and the transfer, to local electoral councils and the IFE, of oversight of the process whereby incoming congresses vote to approve their own election. The PRI also agreed that the voter rolls would be verified by an independent body. The opposition failed to gain PRI concessions in two significant areas: first, no limits were placed on public functionaries' direct involvement in electoral campaigning; and second, parties were not blocked from using the colors of the national flag as their own.[5] The government later agreed to make further reforms after the Zapatista National Liberation Army rebelled in Chiapas on January 1, 1994. This final

---

[3] Originally the PRI proposed that the fourth senatorship would only be awarded in those cases where the second party had a significantly strong showing (the PRI suggested a threshold of 25 percent of the vote). However, in its final form, the reform included no minimum threshold. Increasing the number of Senate seats was a clever tactic in that it reduces the likelihood of PAN-PRD coalition candidates. Henceforth, each party will want to compete for the fourth senatorial spot. Even where the PRI loses the direct elections in a state, it would always expect to come in second and, therefore, seems almost certain to continue to enjoy a large majority in the Senate.

[4] No party will be able to obtain more than 63 percent of the seats in Congress. Therefore, any party wishing to propose constitutional changes will have to build an alliance with at least one other party.

[5] This is obviously aimed at the PRI, whose colors and their relative positions are identical to those of the national flag and to government programs like the National Solidarity Program. For more on this conflation of PRI-government nationalism, see Rodríguez and Ward 1994a. It seems likely that in the long term the PRI will also concede on this point, but only after it has accustomed its traditional followership to a new set of colors—not something the PRI felt it could accomplish in the twelve months prior to the 1994 elections.

phase of concessions included changes to the IFE and a pledge to allow international observers to monitor elections.[6]

The most important change in the electoral structure to be put in place by the August 1994 federal elections was the recomposition of the General Council of the Federal Electoral Institute, the highest authority overseeing polling and vote tabulation. In 1994 for the first time, neither the PRI nor the federal government controlled the council. Of its eleven voting seats, six were held by nonpartisan "citizen counselors" and four by legislators from the three principal parties (two by the PRI and one each by the PRD and the PAN). Finally, although the president of the General Council (still the interior minister) also has a vote, he can no longer cast his vote to break a tie. Significantly, these last-minute proposals originated with the opposition. They were endorsed by the three principal political parties and, generally speaking, were lauded by political analysts (see Alcocer 1994: 47), though some questioned the advisability of replacing "judge counselors" with less-qualified "citizen counselors" (Farías Mackey, in Ward et al. 1994: 29–31).

It is not only within the Congress that pluralist representation expanded. From 1982 onward, opposition parties won a significant number of city governments. Some of these victories—including the Mexican Democratic Party's (PDM) triumph in Guanajuato and that of the Socialist Workers' Party (PST) in Ensenada, both in 1983—appear to have been orchestrated by the PRI in an effort to promote a semblance of democracy (Rodríguez and Ward 1992). Others occurred when splits within the PRI over candidate selection left the door wide open for an opposition party victory. Still other opposition successes in 1983 occurred in important northern cities—such as Zamora, Hermosillo, Agua Prieta, Durango, Ciudad Juárez, and Chihuahua—where López Portillo's expropriation of the banking system produced a massive swing of the business sector away from the PRI and to the PAN (Mizrahi 1994; Rodríguez and Ward 1992). In addition to these PAN wins, Dr. Salvador Nava Martínez won the municipal presidency of San Luis Potosí for the Frente Cívico Potosino. In combination, these gains were significant not only because the opposition got control of important population centers, but also because they signaled a new era in electoral competition in which opposition municipal presidency and federal deputyship victories would be recognized. One PAN official recalled, "It was like Switzerland up there. There was no interference in the voting, and the ballot count was absolutely clean" (in Cornelius 1987: 22). De la Madrid's

---

[6]Senior government officials' support for this proposal softened somewhat over time as they cited the insufficient interval allowed for effective implementation. Nevertheless, the 1994 elections were watched by national observers recruited from among partisans and nonpartisans alike and trained in campaign and election monitoring. Observers were drawn from the National Union of Education Workers (SNTE) and from NGOs such as Alianza Cívica.

experiment in system opening was short-lived, however; in 1985 and 1986 the PRI regained control of most of these cities, though not necessarily by fair means (Bezdek 1995; Rodríguez and Ward 1992). These elections, coming midway in de la Madrid's presidential term, were among the most blatantly fraudulent in recent Mexican history. It was a question of one step forward, two steps back.

After Salinas's inauguration as president in 1988, opposition victories multiplied, and opposition parties were often able to retain control of municipalities through consecutive terms—for example, in San Luis Potosí, León, San Pedro Garza García, Ensenada, and Tijuana. In 1993 more than two hundred municipal governments were in the hands of the opposition, and over half of these were controlled by the PAN (Cornelius 1994).

The PAN also made electoral breakthroughs at the state level—in Baja California in 1989 and in Chihuahua in 1992. Elsewhere, disputed electoral outcomes and postelection civil disturbances forced Salinas to remove winning gubernatorial candidates, despite the fact that, under the Mexican constitution, it is the Senate and not the executive which is empowered to remove a governor and select a replacement governor from a list of three candidates offered by the president.[7] This gave the PAN a third governorship, that of Guanajuato in 1991. In other notable cases—such as San Luis Potosí, Michoacán, Tabasco, and Yucatán—interim PRI governors were installed. This construction of pluralism from above through presidential fiat demonstrates that presidentialism and centralism remain entrenched within the political system and that the process of selecting and electing PRI candidates is far from democratic. Only in contexts such as Chihuahua and Baja California, where the opposition governs, are the "metaconstitutional" powers of the president less effective. Where the president does not control the party in power, he cannot remove the constitutionally elected governor and appoint his personal choice to the governorship. In extreme circumstances, of course, the president could press the Senate to declare an annulment of government (*inexistencia de poderes*) in order to effect a replacement, but there would have to be sufficient grounds to ensure public compliance; political expediency would not suffice.

Opening has also taken place in Mexico's civic culture and process. Clientelistic relations between community/labor groups and PRI politicians/government officials have declined, to be replaced by more systematic and routinized patterns of interaction (Ward 1986)—though some would argue that Salinas's Solidarity Program has turned the clock

---

[7]The Senate rarely exercises this function since the governor or governor-elect invariably agrees to "resign" or to take extended leave if pressed to do so by the president. This is but one element of the "metaconstitutional" powers enjoyed by Mexican presidents, which arise from the almost total domination of executive over legislative powers (Garrido 1989: 422–24).

back toward populism and clientelism (Dresser 1991; but compare Cornelius, Craig, and Fox 1994). Powerful bosses in principal labor unions, such as the SNTE and the petroleum workers' union, were either removed or undermined by President Salinas, and, generally speaking, unions today offer more democratic representation for their members (Cook 1990). Residents' associations and community organizations are also more likely to be headed by democratically elected leaders (Foweraker and Craig 1990). There has been an opening of the press, particularly among national weekly publications such as *Este País* and *Voz y Voto*. Also, since 1988, the media have been much more open in publicizing the results of opinion polls conducted by partisan and nonpartisan organizations. Most important of all, several national movements have emerged with the purpose of monitoring and protecting the vote at elections, defending the democratic advances that have been won, and denouncing any attempt by the regime to interfere with these advances; examples are Convergencia, which includes Ola por la Democracia (Chihuahua) and Movimiento Ciudadano para la Democracia (which originated in San Luis Potosí in 1991 and later extended to the national level), the Alianza Cívica, etc. Finally, there has been growing resolve in the area of civil rights, although advances to date have been confined almost exclusively to human rights issues.[8]

In 1989, President Salinas created the National Human Rights Commission, which has made some progress in reducing human rights abuses nationwide. However, the commission has not been free of problems: its first two attorneys general were removed because of incompetence or outright abuse of office; the commission's first president left this post for another in 1992; and in May 1994 the commission's fourth attorney general resigned after failing to make significant headway against a corrupt judiciary and organized crime. Despite its efforts to combat human rights abuses, the Salinas administration's record in the arena of political rights is not good: although the exact numbers are disputed, on the order of two hundred PRD militants are estimated to have died in politically motivated conflicts and assassinations during Salinas's term in office (Cornelius 1994: 63).

While indicative of an important opening on the political playing field, all of these processes—political liberalization, growing pluralism, more openness for civic participation—do not necessarily add up to democratization. The period since 1968 has been characterized as one of "transition," as Mexico moves away from the traditional political and social order built around revolutionary principles (Aguilar Camín and Meyer 1993; Barros Horcasitas, Hurtado, and Pérez Fernández 1991). But

---

[8]Civil rights such as the right to vote and the right to organize do not fall within the mandate of the National Human Rights Commission. However, Baja California created its state-level Human Rights Commission *before* the federal commission came into existence, and the state entity is empowered with a much broader mandate.

does this political transition also constitute a *democratic* transition? That is the question which we propose to examine in the remainder of this book for the specific case of Baja California.

Shortly after taking office, Salinas indicated his commitment to change—not least in his willingness to recognize Ernesto Ruffo's gubernatorial victory in Baja California. Nevertheless, in many respects Salinas found economic change more easily accomplished than political reform. Reform of Mexico's political process has always stopped short of allowing an alternation in power at the federal level, and several factors suggest that the most fertile ground for democratic opening is still the outer reaches of the country, particularly in the north. Northern Mexico is known for its independence from the center, due largely to its considerable per capita wealth, relatively high education levels, proximity to the United States and U.S. culture, and a weaker pattern of domination by the PRI's corporate structure.

Guillén López recently suggested that the principal measure of democratic transition in Baja California is the possibility for parties to alternate in government (Guillén López 1993). This *alternancia* remains the dominant characteristic of the state's "democratic transition," even though Guillén López acknowledges that the state's institutional structures also must change. If they do not, then the process is a political transition rather than a democratic change. Although we concur with Guillén López in that there are many caveats and contradictions in any attempt to sustain the argument for genuine democratic change, ours is a more positive interpretation, particularly insofar as we give greater credence to the separation of powers between the executive and the legislative branches (chapter 4) and to the heightened autonomy of both state and municipal governments in the conduct of intergovernmental relations (chapter 5).

In formulating his definition of democratization, Guillén López identifies (and analyzes) three areas of transformation in regional politics since 1989: (1) a redefinition of government structure, particularly insofar as a greater plurality of actors and institutions is concerned; (2) the debilitation and disintegration of traditional corporative structures, as well as their alienation and distancing from state government; and (3) a rearticulation of state-society relations (1993: 30–31). Earlier we outlined the broad dimensions that our analysis will take in chapters 2 through 5, but we, too, believe that democratization is much more than electoral competition and the alternation in power of different parties. A definition of democratization must also embrace features such as the institutionalization of democratic processes; accountability and transparency in government; a free press; respect for civil rights; and the development of a democratic culture which emphasizes participation and not dependency, and which promotes opportunities for new forms of organization and leadership. Our assessment of how these have been achieved in Baja California is contained in the following chapters. However, before we can proceed with the details of our research, it is necessary to contextualize the social, political, and economic setting in which these events have taken place.

Baja California: Geography and Politics in the Periphery

Physical Geography

The state of Baja California is located in northwestern Mexico, on the upper half of the Baja California Peninsula. It is bordered on the north by the United States, on the northeast by the Mexican state of Sonora, and on the south by Baja California Sur. The state's western coastline begins at the U.S.-Mexico border near San Diego and runs south along the Pacific Ocean for 740 kilometers. Its eastern coastline begins at the point where the Colorado River enters the Gulf of California and continues south for 400 kilometers.

Several mountain ranges extend down the center of Baja California. These rugged, granite mountains divide the state into diverse geographic and ecological environments. The western coastal plain, nearly unbroken from north to south, is severely limited in breadth by the mountain ranges which form the spine of the Baja California Peninsula. Mountains also limit the width of the eastern coastal plain, with the exception of the flatlands in the Río Colorado Valley. In many areas the mountains abut the ocean, creating a dramatic scenery of cliffs, isolated beaches, and, along the eastern coastline on the Gulf of California, a number of small islands. Significantly, though, Baja California lacks the resource base of precious metals and other minerals found in many mountainous regions of northern Mexico. Climatically, too, much of this area is desert, with high summer temperatures, a wide diurnal temperature range, and relatively little rainfall.

The rugged landscape and the severe shortages of rainfall over most of the peninsula historically have restricted agriculture to a few river basins. Baja California's two largest cities, Tijuana and Mexicali, are located on two of the state's largest rivers, the Río Tijuana and the Río Colorado, respectively. The introduction of modern irrigation techniques in the Mexicali Valley, through which the Río Colorado flows, has transformed once arid land into commercially profitable agricultural fields. Irrigation has led to such intensive development that the valley shows up in satellite pictures as a multicolored checkerboard of large agricultural plots. The state's third-largest city, Ensenada, is an important port on the Pacific Coast.

This combination of physical geography and peripheral location were not conducive to the state's economic development, at least not until tourism and irrigation offered new possibilities for a viable economic base. Indeed, Baja California was of so little consequence to the center that it was not granted statehood until 1952.

Historical and Political-Administrative Development

Approximately seventy thousand indigenous people inhabited Baja California prior to the arrival of the Spaniards. Hernán Cortés sent an expedition to explore the region around 1534 and in 1535 founded a short-lived colony around a bay he named Santa Cruz. There were many subsequent attempts to colonize the peninsula, in part because of Cortés's discovery of pearls in La Paz Bay (Alvarez 1989; Musacchio 1989). The Jesuits founded the first permanent settlement in 1697 but were expelled from the region seventy years later by the Spanish crown, to be replaced, first, by the Franciscans and shortly thereafter by the Dominicans. This period coincided with heightened Spanish interest in the conquest of the Californias. However, although Spanish military forces used the area as a base for operations, the Baja California Peninsula itself was of little political importance (Alvarez 1989).

In the nineteenth century the peninsula felt the impacts—both military and economic—of the proximity of the United States. During the Mexican War (1846–1848) American troops occupied the cities of La Paz and San José del Cabo, and the United States laid claim to the entire peninsula for annexation (it returned it to Mexico in the peace treaty). Business interests came as well. The Connecticut-based International Company of Mexico was influential in the area, particularly in Ensenada's early urban development (Alvarez 1989; Musacchio 1989). In 1890 the company ceded its interests to the Mexican Colonization Company, which soon gained control over much of the area's economy. Mexicali began attracting American investment because of its combination of mild climate and proximity to the Río Colorado, suiting it well for intensive agricultural production.

When Mexicali was attacked by anti-Porfirian forces in 1911, American proponents of annexation viewed this as an opportunity to gain more territory for the United States. However, their efforts toward this end were forestalled by protests from the Mexican government and by intervention from the U.S. government (Alvarez 1989). The peninsula fell under control of different factions during the Mexican Revolution; it was later divided into two districts, each headed by a governor appointed by the federal government. Mexicali was made the capital of the northern district in 1928. The two districts became territories in 1931; in 1952 Baja California was made a state, and in 1953 its constitution entered into effect (Alvarez 1989).

Administratively, the state is divided into four municipalities. The areal extent of two of these is extremely limited and corresponds almost entirely to the urban areas of present-day Tijuana and Tecate. Mexicali (the state capital) and Ensenada are very large municipal entities, both with extensive rural hinterlands. Politically, the state is divided on the basis of population into fifteen state congressional districts. (The state congress is unicameral.) Mexicali and Tijuana, with their much larger populations, command six districts each; Ensenada has two, and Tecate, one. A different configuration of these districts provides the basis for the federal electoral districts which elect six deputies to the national legislature. Like all other Mexican states, Baja California had until 1994 elected two members to the federal Senate.

Population and Urbanization

Prior to the 1910–1917 Mexican Revolution, Baja California was almost entirely undeveloped, with a small population. Today, at least in per capita terms, it is one of the wealthiest states in Mexico. Its two largest cities, Tijuana and Mexicali, have been transformed from small rural settlements into major economic centers. The economy of Tijuana is dominated by tourism and *maquiladora* (in-bond assembly) industries, while Mexicali lies within one of the most productive agricultural regions in Mexico. Both cities experienced dramatic population increases after the 1950s, fueled by their proximity to the U.S.-Mexico border and the opportunities offered by their expanding economies.

The population of the state increased nearly 220 percent between 1960 and 1990 (from 520,165 to over 1.6 million), compared to the 133 percent increase experienced by Mexico as a whole over the same period (see table 1.1). This growth occurred almost entirely in urban areas (table 1.2). Much of this statewide increase was due to immigration. Indeed, the expanding frontiers of economic opportunity in the state, as well as its location as a stopping-off point for labor migration into the United States, have meant that immigration remains an important component of Baja California's growth (Chávez Galindo 1987). In 1940, 55 percent of the population was born outside of the state; although this figure had declined to 40 percent by 1980, immigrants still constitute about one-third of the total population. Most of this incoming population comes from other Mexican states, principally Jalisco and the southern states of Oaxaca and Chiapas (Chávez Galindo 1987: 9–11; Pick, Butler, and Lanzer 1987: 106). In recent years, it appears that significant numbers of non-Mexican nationals have come to Baja California as well, usually Central Americans traveling up through Mexico (Chávez Galindo 1987: 9).[9]

Urban development in Mexicali, Tijuana, and Ensenada has been shaped by three forces: (1) the economic opportunities resulting from its proximity to the United States; (2) substantial population growth due to

---

[9]While Baja California has been populated largely through in-migration, there is an enormous throughflow of population, such that the net rate of migration is relatively low (0.3 percent, according to data cited in Pick, Butler, and Lanzer 1987). In part, therefore, Baja California (and Tijuana, in particular) is a region of sojourners (Stephen 1991).

TABLE 1.1
POPULATION GROWTH BY STATE, MUNICIPALITY,
AND PRINCIPAL URBAN CENTER, 1960–1990

	1960	1970	% Increase	1980	% Increase	1990	% Increase
Baja California State	520,165	870,421	67	1,177,886	35	1,660,885	41
Municipality							
Ensenada	64,934	115,423	78	175,435	52	259,979	48
Mexicali	281,333	396,324	41	510,664	29	601,938	18
Tecate	8,208	18,091	120	30,540	69	51,557	69
Tijuana	165,690	340,583	106	461,257	35	747,381	62
City							
Ensenada	42,561	77,687	83	120,483	55	169,426	41
Mexicali	174,540	263,498	51	341,559	30	438,377	28
Tecate	6,588	14,738	124	23,909	62	40,240	68
Tijuana	152,374	277,306	82	429,500	55	698,752	63

Source: INEGI, *Censo General de Población de los Estados Unidos Mexicanos, 1969–1990* (Mexico City: INEGI).

TABLE 1.2
RURAL AND URBAN POPULATION BY MUNICIPALITY, 1960–1990

	1960		1990		% Change 1960–1990	
	Rural	Urban	Rural	Urban	Rural	Urban
Baja California State	116,102	404,063	151,061	1,509,794	30	274
Municipality						
Ensenada	9,835	45,099	46,006	213,973	368	374
Mexicali	84,257	197,076	85,425	516,513	1.4	162
Tecate	1,620	6,588	11,317	40,240	599	511
Tijuana	10,390	155,300	8,313	739,068	–20	376

Source: INEGI, *Censo General de Población de los Estados Unidos Mexicanos, 1969–1990* (Mexico City: INEGI).

immigration, which created a high demand for land and housing; and (3) federal government investment in physical infrastructure to facilitate foreign investment and stimulate tourism (Herzog 1990). In terms of the growth of the individual municipalities, Mexicali has grown the least; indeed, its substantial rural population grew hardly at all between 1960 and 1990 (table 1.2). Even though it still has a population of over a half-million people, Mexicali has ceded its position as the state's principal urban center to Tijuana. The fact that Mexicali remains dominated by agricultural interests is an important feature for understanding that city's politics and voting patterns, as will be discussed in later chapters. Ensenada's rural population has grown substantially, as has Tecate's, but

TABLE 1.3

SERVICE DEFICITS FOR DWELLINGS IN BAJA CALIFORNIA BY MUNICIPALITY, 1970–1990

Year	Municipality	Number of Dwellings	% without Potable Water	% without Sewerage	% without Electricity
1970	Ensenada	21,245	39	59	NA
	Mexicali	68,175	28	61	NA
	Tecate	3,195	45	47	NA
	Tijuana	63,244	36	52	NA
1980	Ensenada	35,993	28	41	18
	Mexicali	99,561	13	33	8
	Tecate	6,216	39	44	26
	Tijuana	96,833	28	33	11
1990	Ensenada	60,070	18	36	16
	Mexicali	135,732	13	32	6
	Tecate	11,550	30	38	23
	Tijuana	166,124	33	37	17
1970	Baja California	155,859	33	57	NA
1980	Baja California	238,603	22	34	11
1990	Baja California	373,476	23	35	13

Source: INEGI, *Censo General de Población de los Estados Unidos Mexicanos, 1969–1990* (Mexico City: INEGI).

these increases are upon very low initial base levels and reflect rising economic opportunities in tourism and agricultural production, respectively. Tijuana has become the single most important urban center, having grown twice as fast as Mexicali (tables 1.1 and 1.2; Herzog 1990). Today, events and processes in Tijuana exert disproportionate influence on the state.

One important outcome of this rapid urbanization has been the pressure put on state and municipal authorities to house and provide urban services for the population. In Baja California overall, the proportion of dwellings without water and sewer connections declined significantly between 1970 and 1990 (table 1.3).[10] Disaggregated by municipality (*municipio*) and taking water provision as an example, it is clear that Tijuana continues to experience major deficits (around one-third of all dwellings lack services), and although the city has extended water provision to a large number of households in absolute terms, the utility service agencies are clearly running fast just to maintain the existing

---

[10] It is widely acknowledged that the 1980 population census data are not reliable. They overestimate the population and exaggerate the level of infrastructure provision (Connolly 1993). Care should be taken, therefore, when using these data.

level of servicing. Mexicali, with its slower rate of urbanization, has managed to reduce relative deficits significantly (from 28 percent to 13 percent). Ensenada, too, appears to be coping rather well with its program of service provision (table 1.3). These features of servicing deficits provide important contextual material for our later analysis of state and municipal administrations and their respective priorities in development programs.

The Baja California Economy

The economy of Baja California is surprisingly diverse, given physical geography and the political changes the state has undergone since the early part of this century. Transformed from an isolated, arid ranching community into an industrial and agricultural center, Baja California includes five major sectors of economic activity: agriculture, fishery, industry, commerce, and services (including tourism) (Baja California 1987, 1989; INEGI 1991). Tijuana accounts for over half the state's gross domestic product (GDP), largely because it contains most of the *maquiladora* manufacturing (table 1.4). Mexicali's importance, while considerable, is a far second.

- The agriculture sector has expanded continuously since the 1950s and now accounts for around 34 percent of the state's GDP—most of it (91 percent) concentrated in Mexicali (Nolasco 1989: 212). Agriculture, livestock raising, and forestry together form the most important sector in terms of revenues generated—mostly from irrigated farming in the Mexicali Valley and seasonal farming in the coastal zone. While the coastal zone is larger, the irrigated Mexicali Valley is more important for the production of fruits, vegetables, and grains for export. Three regions produce beef, pork, and dairy products: the Mexicali region, the eastern coastal plain, and the region stretching from Ensenada to Baja California Sur. Forestry is relatively unimportant to the state's economy.

- Fishing off the coasts of Baja California has expanded in recent years and contributes around 17 percent of the state GDP. The principal locus is Ensenada (accounting for 90 percent of GDP generated by this sector [Nolasco 1989: 70]), but other notable fishing centers include San Felipe, Isla de Cedros, San Quintín, El Rosario, Villa de Jesús María, Isla de Guadalupe, and Bahía de los Angeles. In 1986, 23 percent of the total volume of the catch was exported, but this portion accounted for 71 percent of the catch's total value. The commercial potential of this sector is of considerable importance to the state, prompting federal government support through the Banco Nacional Pesquero y Portuario, which has helped build and operate regional storage facilities and ice plants (Baja California 1987; 1989).

TABLE 1.4
RATE OF GDP GROWTH BY SECTOR, 1940–1980

		%
1940–1950	Total	4.4
	Agriculture/Fish/Food	1.4
	Industry	5.3
	Services	1.2
1950–1960	Total	6.9
	Agriculture/Fish/Food	4.6
	Industry	6.6
	Services	7.8
1960–1970	Total	8.9
	Agriculture/Fish/Food	8.3
	Industry	9.4
	Services	8.9
1970–1980	Total	3.0
	Agriculture/Fish/Food	3.0
	Industry	5.2
	Services	3.5

Source: A. Sánchez Pérez, "Estructura y dinámica del sector manufacturero baja californiano (1960–1985)," *Cuadernos de Ciencias Sociales* (Universidad Autónoma de Baja California), Series 3.

- The industrial sector has absorbed some of the labor displaced by the adoption of capital-intensive production techniques in agriculture and fishing. *Maquiladoras* account for much of the state's industrial development since the 1960s, although other industries (producing foods and beverages, furniture, clothing and textiles, metal products, construction materials, chemicals, agricultural machinery, and assembling automobiles) have also developed and received government support. Nevertheless, the *maquiladoras* remain a key component of the industrial sector (Sklair 1993). They bring foreign currency into the state and create a large number of jobs in the major cities. Tijuana accounts for roughly one-half of the industrial concentration in Baja California; Mexicali represents about one-third. Of the remaining industry, approximately 85 percent is located in Ensenada and 15 percent in Tecate (Baja California 1987, 1989). In terms of state GDP (minus border transfers), the industrial sector generates around 38 percent of the total (table 1.4). A broad indication of the type of manufacturing activities undertaken in each municipality is provided in table 1.5.

- The business sector's primary concern has been to provide the state with an adequate supply of basic goods to satisfy regional consump-

TABLE 1.5
BROAD INDUSTRIAL SUBSECTORS BY MUNICIPALITY, 1984

Rank	Ensenada	Mexicali	Tecate	Tijuana
1	Food/beverage	Construction	*Maquiladoras*	*Maquiladoras*
2	Construction	Machinery	Machinery	Food/beverage
3	*Maquiladoras*	Food/beverage	Wood products	Construction
4	Machinery	Paper/printing	Food/beverage	Wood products

Source: A. Sánchez Pérez, "Estructura y dinámica del sector manufacturero baja californiano (1960–1985)," *Cuadernos de Ciencias Sociales* (Universidad Autónoma de Baja California), Series 3.

tion needs. Regional production has never come close to meeting regional demand, and neighboring states have not been able to compensate entirely for the shortfall. This situation has compelled merchants to rely on imports, especially since Lázaro Cárdenas instituted a duty-free zone in Baja California in 1937. The business sector is second only to industry in terms of generating new employment opportunities in the state (Baja California 1987, 1989; INEGI 1991).

• The services sector is another significant element in the state economy, primarily because of the importance of tourism. There has been steady growth in the number of annual visitors to Baja California, and revenues from tourism have increased concomitantly. The government provides substantial support to this sector, primarily through FONATUR credits (Baja California 1987, 1989). Tourism is largely restricted to the border area, which attracted 80 percent of the state's visitors in 1984, although Tijuana's dominance in tourism began to decline toward the end of the 1980s as tourists ventured further inland, especially to the newly developed recreational facilities along the Ensenada coast. Overall, the services sector produces around 11 percent of state GDP. Despite this relatively small contribution, services employ the bulk of the economically active population (table 1.6).

The Economically Active Population

The total active labor force—or economically active population (EAP)—includes people over twelve years of age who are either already working or seeking employment. The EAP in Baja California grew from 167,436 in 1960 to 403,279 in 1980. The percentage of the EAP participating in agriculture, livestock raising, and fishery decreased from 1960 to 1980, while the percentage participating in industry and services increased. This change mirrors the nature of Baja California's development process over the past thirty years. In 1960, the most important economic activity was agriculture, but by 1980, industry (especially the *maquiladoras*) and

Table 1.6
Economically Active Population by Sector and Municipality, 1980
(percent)

	Agriculture, Fishery, & Food	Industry	Services
Ensenada	15	11	42
Mexicali	14	11	42
Tecate	10	21	36
Tijuana	3	17	46

Source: INEGI, Censo General de Población de los Estados Unidos Mexicanos, 1980 (Mexico City: INEGI).

services (primarily tourism) had become the driving forces behind the state's economic prosperity (INEGI 1986). Moreover, associated with these two leading economic edges, the female participation rate increased from 17 percent to 30 percent between 1960 and 1980 (Baja California 1989).

Not counted in these statistics are the many Mexican nationals who move within and across the border region on a daily basis for employment purposes. These "border commuters," who represent a significant proportion of the economically active population, cross into the United States to work—primarily in unskilled and semiskilled services, such as the hotel industry and automobile repair (Herzog 1990). It is estimated that Tijuana and Mexicali had a combined total of 20,676 border commuters in 1970, a figure that had increased to 56,319 by 1980. Indeed, the number of border commuters in 1980 even surpassed the number of workers employed in Tijuana and Mexicali *maquiladoras*. In 1980 the border area—comprising Tijuana, Mexicali, and Tecate—accounted for 85 percent of the state's economically active population (Nolasco 1989: 212–14).

The swelling urban population, the economic shift away from agriculture to industry and services, and the relatively higher educational level of Baja California's population[11] have led to the growth of an urban middle class in the state. However, only 28,603 individuals, or 7 percent of the EAP, were employed as professionals, technical specialists, or private-sector managers in 1980 (Nolasco 1989: 38).

Labor and Community Organizations

The rapid population growth and the changing pattern of Baja California's economic development have altered the state's social structure dramatically, particularly the composition of the most significant interest groups. Labor unions have had a presence in Baja California since

---

[11] Enrollment in institutes of higher education rose from 111 in 1969 to 19,786 in 1990 (Lorey 1990: 99).

1907, when public transport workers and casino workers organized unions. The Nationalist League (Liga Nacionalista), most visible in the workers' and migrants' urban center of Colonia Libertad in Tijuana, was formed around 1925 to represent carpenters, musicians, and restaurant workers—contributing significantly to the politicization of the region's workers (Bustamante 1985: 318).

In more recent years the most important unions in Baja California, representing construction, transport, and industrial workers, have come to be controlled by central federations like the Revolutionary Confederation of Workers and Peasants (CROC) and the Confederation of Mexican Workers (CTM). The CROC and the CTM appear to be the strongest unions, followed by the Regional Confederation of Mexican Workers (CROM) and the Revolutionary Confederation of Workers (CRT). The CROC controls the most powerful local union, the "Red Dawn" (Alba Roja), while the CTM represents workers in the cotton, meat-processing, and petroleum industries (Salas-Porras Soulé 1989: 73). Although much of the literature on unions and women's organizations focuses almost exclusively on the *maquiladora* industry in Tijuana and Mexicali, union organization in this sector tends to be minimal (Carrillo V. 1985: 153; Sklair 1993).

Urban popular movements have had a strong presence in Baja California since the 1940s. In 1978, the Committee of Urban Neighborhoods of Tijuana (COCUTAC) was founded; this organization was responsible for organizing land invasions of four neighborhoods and eventually included a consumer cooperative and a clinic (Valenzuela Arce 1987: 27). Women have been active in the state's urban popular movements. The Women's Neighborhood Group (Grupo Femenino de Colonias) was a pressure group representing the interests of poor neighborhoods and promoting the development of public works, clinics, and adult education (Price 1973: 72). Both the internal organization of these labor and community groups, as well as their intimate association with the PRI, have changed dramatically since the PAN won control of the state in 1989.

The Rise of the Opposition in Baja California

As noted at the beginning of this overview, Baja California was passed around, taken over, given up, and, finally, gathered into the Mexican federation. But attaining statehood did not close the book on the state's rather ambivalent political history; it merely began a new chapter. Its newness, its relative unimportance (especially in the earlier period), and, above all, its location away from the mainstream of federal life have all combined to allow, first, for the emergence of a long series of inept and often corrupt governors and, second, for the growth of a strong regional opposition constructed around the PAN.

Baja California's first governor, Braulio Maldonado Sánchez, was an imposed candidate. His administration (1953–1959) was characterized by assassinations, vice, and fraud; the governor personally had interests in prostitution and gambling, and he maintained a group of gunmen known as "Los Chemitas." Maldonado's corruption and use of intimidation were significant factors in the emergence of support for opposition parties in the state.

The PAN has been the strongest opposition party in Baja California since 1943, when it first established a regional office in the territory. Although the PAN participated in the first state election in 1953, the state and local elections of August 1959 marked the party's first real foray into electoral competition and set the tone for its experiences over the next thirty years. The PAN made a very strong showing in the elections (many observers felt that it won the governorship), but the PRI stole the elections through massive fraud and carried out violent attacks against the PANistas.

The PAN's failure to make electoral progress early on and indecision among the national party leadership about what role the PAN should play meant that little headway was made locally during the 1960s. In 1973, the state-level party leadership declared electoral competition to be a waste of time and abstained from that year's federal congressional elections, infuriating the PAN national executive committee, which ousted the state leaders and installed a new regional executive committee. The PAN went on to make a poor showing in the 1974 state and local elections, as well as in the 1976 federal elections. However, when the PRI imposed a very unpopular candidate, Hermenegildo Cuenca Díaz, for the 1977 gubernatorial election, the PAN seized the moment to once again run its own candidate.[12]

Interestingly, the first opposition party to win power in Baja California was not the PAN but the Socialist Workers' Party (PST). For the September 1983 elections, the PRI had passed over David Ojeda Ochoa[13] in favor of Jorge Swain to run for Ensenada's municipal presidency. (Swain, former head of the city's public works office, had left this post under a cloud and was very unpopular with the local electorate.) The disaffected Ojeda Ochoa left the PRI for the PST and successfully challenged Swain under the PST banner. Ojeda Ochoa's victory typifies the opposition's past pattern of occasional successes, winning office only when the PRI was split or was particularly disenchanted with a candidate imposed by party higher-ups.

---

[12] Cuenca Díaz commanded the troops who fired on PANista protesters during the 1959 state elections. He died before the 1977 election was held and was replaced by PRI candidate Roberto De Lamadrid, who won the governorship.

[13] Ojeda Ochoa had been Ensenada's first municipal president (under the PRI's banner) after Baja California attained statehood in 1952.

Both former governor Roberto De Lamadrid (1977–1983) and his successor, Xicoténcatl Leyva Mortera (1983–1989), were particularly inept as governors of Baja California. In reaction to their poor performance, the state went firmly in favor of Cardenista Front candidate Cuauhtémoc Cárdenas in the 1988 presidential election. This protest vote, provoked largely by widespread dissatisfaction with Leyva, forced Salinas to replace him with an interim governor, Oscar Baylón. Perhaps it was the inauspicious performance of De Lamadrid and Leyva which persuaded Salinas that the PRI should not use untoward tactics to defeat widely renowned PANista Ernesto Ruffo Appel in Baja California's 1989 gubernatorial election. Ruffo's victory required Salinas's sanction to become official, and this approval was forthcoming, again probably because the poor status of the PRI's image in the state left the president little room for maneuver. Another factor was the state's peripheral location: if the center was going to experiment with an opposition government at the state level, then better to test the waters in outer regions, particularly where an "open and fair" election could be showcased to the United States. The following chapters assess that experiment.

2

Democratization through *Alternancia* and the Changing Electoral Process

The statewide elections held in Baja California on July 2, 1989, marked a watershed in the process of democratization that has been unfolding by fits and starts over the past decade or so, both in the state and in Mexico as a whole. In the context of a national process of political liberalization, the elections in Baja California were viewed as significant because the victory of the National Action Party's candidate, Ernesto Ruffo, marked the first time in sixty years of one-party rule in Mexico that a gubernatorial election was conceded to an opposition party. First and foremost, the Institutional Revolutionary Party's concession of defeat was a sign to the political community that President Salinas was willing to allow a state government to fall into the hands of the opposition. Putting aside for the moment the controversial issues of how far Salinas might have orchestrated or "controlled" this non-PRI victory, and under what circumstances he might have permitted other opposition successes at the gubernatorial level, Ruffo's victory did have the important effect of energizing the opposition by expanding the realm of what was viewed as politically possible. Second, PANistas viewed Ruffo's election as an opportunity to test the extent to which the principles of federalism—as stated in the constitution—could in fact be put into practice at a higher tier of government than any they had experienced to date (Rodríguez and Ward 1992). In Mexico, where the powers of state governors have traditionally been closely circumscribed by party discipline and by the centralization of power in the hands of the president, the Ruffo administration (and more recently that of Francisco Barrio in Chihuahua) offers a crucial test case for determining the extent to which a state government of the opposition can exercise greater autonomy vis-à-vis the federal government.

The July 1989 elections were also important in the context of emerging democratic processes at the state and local levels in Baja California. The emergence of a more democratic state polity is evident in two principal respects. First, electoral results from the two most recent state elections, in July 1989 and August 1992, highlight sharp increases in party competition between the PAN and the PRI. Second, these elections have brought about opposition control of the state government and some municipal governments, and increased representation of opposition parties in the state congress, giving rise to a government structure that is unique in Mexico. A detailed examination of the impact of that government structure upon inter- and intragovernmental relations, decentralization, and governability issues will be taken up principally in chapters 4 and 5.

In this chapter we focus on elections and the changing electoral processes in Baja California in order to begin our assessment of the real nature and extent of democratization experienced in the region. Specifically, we wish to tie together three major facets of analysis. First, by analyzing electoral trends in Baja California, we propose to evaluate the phenomenon of increasing electoral competition. In order to assess changes in this arena we focus the discussion upon two broad areas. On the one hand, we examine the national and local factors that are responsible for driving the process of political opening (*apertura*) statewide. To anticipate our conclusion, we argue that the process of democratization has been driven by a range of societal pressures—but largely from *within*. While the state's political opposition (most notably, but not exclusively, the PAN) has played a leadership role in the process, for the most part regional political actors and institutions have reacted to societal demands for change. On the other hand, we examine voting patterns themselves. An analysis of spatial voting patterns, demography, and changing voter preferences will help provide a map of the current electoral landscape. Our analysis suggests an emerging electoral structure that has a bipartisan tendency and is both highly competitive and volatile. The lack of strong links between the parties and the electorate, as well as the lack of distinction between partisan agendas, are factors that help account for the voting preferences of an electorate that may prove, ultimately, to be as fickle as any.

The second facet of democratization which we consider points to shifts in the composition of the state congress arising directly from increased electoral competition. The key issue addressed here is whether the current system, which provides for some "opposition" representation in the four *plurinominal* seats (seats assigned proportionately, depending on the respective parties' share of the vote), is entirely consistent with democratic principles or is a carryover from yesteryear, when there was a concern to bolster the appearance of democracy in Mexico without conceding an actual loss of control. We also explore the extent to which the emerging state congress facilitates or hinders governability. Our findings lead us toward conclusions similar to those of other studies which have argued that mechanisms providing for some level of proportional inclusion in congress overrepresent "micro-parties" and thus dilute the strength of the strongest opposition (Molinar Horcasitas 1986; Baer 1990).

The third facet we weigh in analyzing democratization concerns the impact of increased electoral competition upon party linkages with society and upon strategies for attracting voter support. The PRI, confronted with a situation where corporatist organizations no longer work effectively to mobilize the vote, has turned to two alternative strategies. First, recognizing that the traditional practice of imposing candidates from the top down has hindered its competitiveness, the PRI has undertaken some experiments with locally known candidates who have greater grassroots appeal. Second, and with somewhat greater success, the PRI has relied upon the "selective populism" of the National Solidarity Program (PRONASOL) to win back some of the ground lost in 1988 (Cornelius, Craig, and Fox 1994). Our study indicates that PRONASOL support has been solicited by local government officials of both the PAN and the PRI, and that the program is generally viewed in a positive light by the electorate.[1] However, the reliance that both state and local PRIístas appear to place upon PRONASOL as a means of securing electoral support is problematic, for while it is clear that Solidarity helped to reinforce public support for President Salinas, it is not clear that this necessarily translated into more widespread support for candidates of the PRI (Molinar Horcasitas and Weldon 1994).

In short, our purpose is to shed light on a series of issues that are of central importance to this study; namely, to what extent do these new developments represent changes that are consistent with *enduring* democratic government? Do shifting electoral patterns and processes suggest the emergence of a viable system of multiparty competition, with possibilities for alternation of parties in government (*alternancia*)? Are we witnessing the demise of the PRI and the rise of a new era of PAN-dominated politics and government in Baja California? Alternatively, what if the PAN fails to demonstrate to the electorate that it can govern more effectively than its PRIísta predecessors? Will a brief period of PANista rule be followed by a recovery and subsequent retrenchment of the PRI in 1995? Obviously we can only speculate about the future, but our research encourages us to think that we are seeing the tentative first steps toward a more democratic system of genuine multiparty competition and governance—at least in Baja California.

---

[1] In local government at least. Ruffo and other senior executive officers are more circumspect and critical of its politically partisan (PRI) construction, targeting, and appeal (see chapter 3).

Political Transition and Changing Electoral Processes

Since 1989, the political system in Baja California has been undergoing a process of accelerated democratic change. But before turning to an examination of the electoral trends which document these developments, it is important to discuss briefly the forces operating at the state and national levels which have driven this process of democratic transition. As we described earlier, the national trend of political liberalization which was unfolding unsteadily and unevenly in Mexico during the 1980s was driven by an array of factors, including federal electoral reform (Middlebrook 1986); the business community's reaction to the bank nationalization of 1982 (Maxfield 1990); voter discontent with the government's programs of fiscal austerity and economic restructuring (Cornelius, Gentleman, and Smith 1989); the emergence of opposition forces around Cuauhtémoc Cárdenas (Reding 1988); and the pressure on the de la Madrid and Salinas administrations to appear democratic in the eyes of their trading partners (Pastor 1990). Throughout Mexico these factors created new social, economic, and political demands for change which are being articulated through actors, organizations, and institutions in ways that are unique to each community. In this analysis of Baja California we identify five major factors that have driven the political opening in the state and that led to the watershed PAN victory of 1989. First is the long history of the PAN in the state (albeit not as a particularly strong force). Second is the effect of the state's economic and social dynamism in shaping a more "progressive" political culture, which we partly alluded to in chapter 1. Third is the occurrence of splits within traditional elite alliances as a result of economic and political changes over the past decade. Fourth is the demonstration effects from other key electoral contests. And fifth is the combined impact of the events and moods that accompanied the 1989 state elections, especially the widespread antipathy for the PRI after a succession of unimpressive governors.

Events Influencing the 1989 Gubernatorial Victory

In Baja California, as in several other border states, the PAN has a long history of being the principal opposition. In fact, the PAN competed in the first state elections in 1953, the year after the territory was granted statehood. However, despite its long-standing presence, throughout the first three decades of electoral competition in the state the PAN failed to win a single elected office. Although the party was hampered during the 1960s and 1970s by a lack of funds, disagreements within the party leadership, and the government's use of electoral fraud and physical intimidation, the PAN nevertheless continued to receive 20 to 30 percent of the vote totals in state and local elections (Valderrábano 1989: 215–16). Elections in 1968 and 1983 appear to have been particularly close. In the

1968 local elections the PAN claimed on the basis of tally sheets that it had won the municipal presidencies of Tijuana and Mexicali, as well as six of the nine seats in the state congress. It claimed that the ruling party had resorted to electoral fraud, and the elections in these two municipalities were annulled (Simonowitz 1979: 144). In 1983 the PAN made a similar claim to victory in the race for municipal president in Mexicali and once again leveled allegations of electoral fraud against the PRI, although this time the initial electoral results stood. Only after three decades of disappointment did the PAN's persistence finally pay off, when it won its first victory in the municipal elections of 1986. This was the election that gave Ernesto Ruffo the municipal presidency of Ensenada, as well as a seat in the state congress representing Ensenada's 14th district.

Although the PAN did not officially win an election until 1986, its persistence over the years made it the best prepared and most likely vehicle to represent the opposition in the wake of the 1988 presidential election—notwithstanding the fact that the Cárdenas-led National Democratic Front (FDN, forerunner of the Party of the Democratic Revolution [PRD]) actually polled greater support in the state at that time. After four decades of organizing the opposition in the state, the PAN was the party with the most recognition among the electorate. It also had the most resources, was the most developed organizationally, and had firmly established links with the business community and the urban middle class. Moreover, the party was a seasoned competitor in the electoral arena. Compared to some of the newer parties on the left, particularly the PRD, the PAN had greater experience in recruiting candidates, running campaigns, and "protecting the vote" on election day. All these factors worked in the PAN's favor as electoral competition in the state heated up after 1988.

The second factor we have identified as contributing to the political opening in Baja California is the dynamism of the state's economy and society. Baja California is one of the most urban and modernized states in Mexico. This modernization and the emergence of a strong middle class have influenced the development of a political culture in the state which has been characterized as more liberal and more open to the option of multiparty competition (Guillén López 1992: 153). During the 1980s the economy of Baja California expanded rapidly due to its proximity to the United States and to its access to a port on the Pacific. Moreover, the state has successfully attracted investment from both foreign and domestic business, as well as from the Mexican government. For Mexican entrepreneurs, the state offers easy access to U.S. markets; for their North American counterparts, the state represents a prime location for in-bond assembly (*maquiladora*) industries. And the Mexican government, recognizing Baja California's key role as a commercial hub for conducting business with the United States and as an outpost for trade with the Pacific Rim, has channeled large sums of money into projects aimed at developing the state's infrastructure. The opening up of commerce and trade during the mid-1980s and the government's creation of duty-free and investment zones along the border provided the state with optimal benefits for regional and global trade expansion. As we saw in chapter 1, Baja California's economy has grown into one of the strongest in the country. Furthermore, it was able to maintain positive growth rates through most of the 1980s and has had one of the lowest unemployment rates in the country.

In turn, this economic dynamism created one of the largest urban middle classes in Mexico. Moreover, the sectoral composition of the economically active population, coupled with the fact that the state's agricultural sector is more mechanized and more oriented toward international markets than in other parts of the country, has made the population, relatively speaking, less subject to control by corporatist organizations. The state also stands out in the relatively high educational level of its population (CONAPO 1988) and in terms of other basic social indicators; only the Federal District regularly surpasses it. As a result, the urban middle class in Baja California has become a strong political force. Because this social stratum is more urban and more frequently employed in economic activities that are beyond the control of traditional corporatist structures, it also tends to be more politically independent. Disgruntled with the corruption and inefficiency of previous administrations, this segment of the community has come to view the opposition as a real and viable alternative to the PRI. This desire for a political alternative has principally benefited the PAN, particularly since its agenda traditionally appealed to this same middle-class electorate.

A third critical factor behind the political transition in Baja California is the occurrence of splits within the traditional alliances among state elites. The two most important ruptures occurred, on the one hand, between the state government and the political bureaucracy, and on the other, between the state government and the business community (Guillén López 1992: 145). Briefly, these splits had their origins in the economic crisis of the 1980s and in federal efforts at political reform and restructuring. Paramount among the problems that led to a deterioration of ties between the state government and the regional business community were the bank nationalization of 1982, the severe impact of the early 1980s currency devaluation, and the widespread perception that levels of corruption and inefficiency were out of control in the administrations of both Governors Roberto De Lamadrid (1977–1983) and Xicoténcatl Leyva (1983–1989).

Parallel to these deteriorating economic relations between the state and the business community was the erosion of ties between the state government and the key sectors of the PRI's corporate base (the Confederation of Mexican Workers, CTM; the National Peasants' Confederation,

CNC; and the National Confederation of Popular Organizations, CNOP). Fundamentally, the deterioration of these corporatist structures derived from the government austerity programs of the 1980s, which both cut government jobs and restricted wage increases. Dissatisfaction with the state's corporatist organizations allowed other parties, particularly those on the left, to pick up additional electoral support. This shift in voter allegiance was evident in the election of the Socialist Workers' Party candidate David Ojeda Ochoa to the municipal presidency of Ensenada in 1983, as well as in the strong support given to the presidential bid of Cuauhtémoc Cárdenas in 1988. On the other hand, the business community's dissatisfaction with the PRI translated into increased levels of electoral support for the PAN. During the 1980s, shifts in party preference among the private sector became evident in the 1983 elections in Mexicali, the 1986 elections in Ensenada, and, of course, most notably the elections of 1989 (Guillén López 1992: 144).[2]

This leads into a discussion of the fourth factor that has influenced the pace of political transition in the state: the impact that key electoral contests have upon public perceptions concerning the viability of the opposition as an alternative to the PRI. Opposition victories and experiences with non-PRI governments at the local level in Baja California and elsewhere have had an important demonstration effect. There has been a strengthening of the public's perception that elections can be a workable vehicle for exercising political choice, that non-PRI governments may be capable of reasonable government, and that grassroots political organization and initiative can help citizens secure public resources and advance their interests.

The two most important demonstration effects were the case of Ensenada and the phenomenon of *neocardenismo*. With all the attention that has been paid in recent years to Ruffo's win of the gubernatorial election in 1989, the fact that the municipality of Ensenada has been ruled by an opposition government since 1983 is often overlooked. The

---

[2]The general view of the business constituency is to put business first and politics a pragmatic second. Accordingly, although the various business chambers promote the active participation of their members in politics, they try to ensure that their organizations remain neutral. If a party member wants to address a business organization, the chambers are usually willing to offer a forum for discussion but generally do not press their members to attend; nor is it usual practice to endorse a particular party or candidate. The business chambers also claim to lobby only with regard to problems that affect the community at large—for instance, on issues such as broad economic questions and the often vexed question of facilitating border crossings. Furthermore, given the issues that arise, these mobilizational efforts are most often directed toward the federal government rather than to the state or municipal level. This is not to infer that the business community is not involved in local government. On the contrary, at both the state and municipal levels there are many examples of individuals in each party moving from the private sector to the government. But when members of the business community want to take an active role in government, they do so as individuals rather than as members of a particular company or professional organization. For interesting comparative work on Chihuahua, see Mizrahi 1994; on Nuevo León and Sonora, see Guadarrama 1987.

first breakthrough came when PST candidate David Ojeda Ochoa won the municipal presidency of Ensenada in 1983. A popular and charismatic figure who back in the 1950s had been the municipality's first president under the PRI, Ojeda Ochoa could attribute his victory more to his own personality and to popular disgruntlement over the PRI's recent candidate selections than to the PST's strength as an opposition party. Nevertheless, the victory had important aftereffects. Local businessman Ernesto Ruffo was able to benefit from this new evaluation of the electoral process to win for the PAN the municipal presidency in Ensenada in 1986. Despite attempts by the state government to make conditions extremely difficult for Ruffo's administration during its three-year term (1986–1989), his government was able to accomplish a number of its goals. Moreover, his success reinforced public perceptions that opposition governments could actually govern effectively, even when constrained by higher levels of (PRI) government. Perhaps even more important for Ruffo's subsequent political success was his ability to "play the martyr" in the face of systematic and unreasonable persecution from the state government. He seized every opportunity to publicize his battles over the state's allocation of Ensenada's municipal budget, and he exposed budgetary maneuvers by the PRI-dominated congress which appeared to slow the delivery of funding to the municipality. Seen as the opposition's David to the ruling party's Goliath, Ruffo was able to cultivate an image as the leading figure of the opposition. The confrontation between the state government and the Ensenada municipal administration, plus Ruffo's ability to turn this into political capital, are important explanations for much of Ruffo's electoral appeal in the race for the governorship in 1989.

Also important in the 1989 elections was the near triumph of *neocardenismo* in the presidential election of 1988. Baja California was one of the five states won by Cárdenas. As Guillén López (1992: 149) has pointed out, the significance of this event for the state election in 1989 centers on the mobilization and recomposition of the electorate. In Baja California, as in several other states, Cárdenas's candidacy mobilized many voters who had previously withdrawn from the electoral process or who had never participated in it. In addition, the opportunity to vote for a candidate on the left pulled support from the PRI's traditional voting base.[3] In essence, the mobilization of voters in the 1988 campaign had three main effects on the 1989 vote. First, *neocardenismo* expanded the base of the opposition in the state insofar as it engaged new voters in the electoral process. Second, by cutting away at the PRI's vote, the PRD's electoral surge was eventually turned to the benefit of the PAN. And third, when the PRD failed during the 1989 campaign to find candidates

---

[3] Guillén López (1992: 144) calculates that 70 percent of the votes given to Cárdenas in 1988 came from disaffected PRI supporters.

able to capture the imagination of voters who had supported the FDN in 1988, many of these same voters, swept up in "ruffomania," subsequently voted for the PAN, notwithstanding its image as being to the right of the PRI.

Finally, in order to understand the forces influencing the results of the 1989 election, we must focus on certain events surrounding the election itself: the disarray of the PRI coming into the election; the weak organization of the PRD; and the relative cohesion of the PAN behind a locally popular candidate. Approaching the 1989 state elections, the PRI had to overcome several obstacles if it was to win fairly. One was to repair the party's tarnished image in the wake of the corruption and incompetence of the previous governor, Xicoténcatl Leyva.[4] Governor Leyva eventually became such a liability for the PRI that President Salinas removed him from office six months prior to the election. The PRI then moved to repair the party's image by appointing interim governor Oscar Baylón, who entered office emphasizing the need to restore honest and efficient government. Soon after Baylón's arrival, the federal government announced plans to invest 1.5 billion pesos in the state in order to improve urban infrastructure. Although this was not too little, it was certainly too late, and these attempts at rapprochement failed to change public attitudes toward the regime.

Another problem for the PRI was the internal instability stemming from efforts to reform the party. As we mentioned earlier, economic restructuring, political reform, and increased electoral competition on a national scale had placed intense pressures for change upon local PRI organizations. These efforts toward change involved the reformulation of party ties with the corporatist sectors and the business community, revisions in the party's criteria and methods for candidate selection, and so on. Guillén López (1992: 158) points out that an indicator of the internal instability plaguing the PRI during this period was the fact that between December 1988 and July 1989 the party's State Directive Committee (Comité Directivo Estatal) changed its president no less than three times. There was also an intensification of conflicts between the PRI-dominated state and campesino organizations, labor unions, and associations representing various neighborhoods—in part an outcome of the familiar practice of jockeying for position which traditionally accompanies gubernatorial transitions. But the disagreements between the reformist wing and the more traditional wing of the PRI were still more fundamental and, as a result, more protracted.

The selection of Margarita Ortega—a virtual unknown—to run as the PRI's candidate for governor in 1989 did little to alleviate intraparty conflict. Ortega's selection suggested that the Salinas administration

---

[4] Ruffo had dramatized the situation by passing his time sweeping the walkway in front of city hall while awaiting municipal funds. His campaign of "sweep-the-bum-out" populism fueled widespread disgust with the Leyva administration.

would use a firm hand to ensure a state government which was amenable to reform. Personally chosen by President Salinas and running under the campaign slogan "with clean hands," Ortega—an outsider and reformer—was viewed as a threat by more hard-line local political bosses. Indeed, instead of acting as a unifying agent with magical voter appeal, Ortega's candidacy had the effect of driving a wedge between the new wing of the PRI and the more traditional politicians and sectoral leadership (Guillén López 1993: 65). Consequently, the PRI remained divided throughout the campaign, unable to rely on the ability and willingness of sectoral leaders to deliver votes. After the elections, relations between the local PRI and the Central National Committee deteriorated even further (Guillén López 1993: 55).

While this internal warfare severely disadvantaged the PRI, interparty conflict and organizational problems also plagued the PRD and other parties on the left. In the wake of the 1988 elections, the FDN had disintegrated due to infighting among its component parties. As a result, the left lost the momentum that it had gained during the previous year. Although the PRD eventually emerged from the broken coalition, it did so just three months prior to the July 2 state elections. Lacking time, experience, and resources, the PRD fought an uphill battle in trying to recapture the groundswell of support that had allowed Cuauhtémoc Cárdenas to carry the state in 1988. It had two major difficulties. The first stemmed from the fact that a great deal of the FDN's success had rested upon candidate Cárdenas's personal appeal, which did not transfer to candidates like Martha Maldonado in the local setting. The second problem for the PRD was its failure to establish links with those voters who had supported the FDN the previous summer—not surprising, given the party's meager resources and its lack of an established organization in the state.

If disorganization and division characterized the campaigns of the PRI and the parties on the left, the PAN's 1989 campaign was notable for its relatively high degree of accord. While the PAN was not free from internal divisions, the party was able to come to an early compromise on the candidacy of Ernesto Ruffo. Such a consensus was reached due to several factors. For one, Ruffo had solid relations with the business community. In addition, Ruffo was seen by party members as a calm and rational conciliator who would be able to work with the PRI and with different factions of the PAN (Guillén López 1992: 174). Perhaps most important, however, was the fact that Ruffo's three years of conflict with an unpopular PRIísta governor (while Ruffo served as municipal president of Ensenada) had gained him considerable notoriety as a fighter for the opposition. In fact, Ruffo had received so much negative coverage in the local partisan press that he had actually come to symbolize the opposition. Hence the PAN's leadership was confident that Ruffo, the ex-mayor of broom-in-hand fame (see note 4, page 37), would be capable of motivating a solid vote from both inside and outside the PAN.

The PAN also ran an effective campaign capitalizing upon Ruffo's popularity by promoting the idea of "ruffomania." This strategy underscored a number of themes, most notably the censure of the state-level PRI government for its corruption and its failure to improve economic conditions. However, the campaign softened these confrontational elements by also adopting more positive images. For example, the PAN broadcast modern music at its rallies, in part to attract young voters who make up a large percentage of the state's electorate. Indeed, the PAN proved successful in attracting young volunteers from the urban middle class. These volunteers performed a host of tasks in "operation vigilance," the opposition's plan of action to protect the vote on election day.

Electoral Patterns and PANista Performance

The 1989 elections marked a dramatic break with Baja California's status quo ante of PRI-dominated state politics. While in the preceding thirty-six years of contesting elections the PAN had won only one municipal presidency, one single-member-district seat, and a few at-large places in the state congress,[5] in the vote on July 2 the party won the governorship, two of the state's four municipal presidencies (Tijuana and Ensenada), and nine of the fifteen single-member-district seats in the state congress.

The first thing that is evident when looking at the 1989 election results is the marked increase in support for the PAN in the gubernatorial race compared with past years (see table 2.1). In the six previous races for governor, the highest vote total for a PAN candidate had been approximately 36 percent (in 1971, when the PAN ran its longtime leader, Salvador Rosas Magallón). In contrast, in the 1989 election Ruffo received 52 percent of the vote, compared with the PRI's 42 percent and the PPS-PFCRN's 2.5 percent. This represented a dramatic turnaround on earlier races for the governorship in which the PAN had only polled around 30 percent (although this last figure is almost double the PAN's national average in presidential elections).

Also important to note are the 1989 elections for the municipal presidencies (see table 2.2). Most significant was the dramatic reversal in Tijuana, where a 46 percent to 19 percent PRI/PAN split in the 1986 elections turned into a 45 percent/32 percent split in favor of the PAN. The PRI also suffered a significant loss of support in Tecate, which it held by only thirty-two votes! Here the PRI's vote total dropped by 6 percentage points while the PAN's increased by 18 percentage points. In Ruffo's home base of Ensenada, the PAN maintained control over the municipal

---
[5] Although a review of local congressional election results for the 1970s and 1980s indicates that the PAN often ran very close with the PRI in some districts (in 1971, for example). Also, the number of annulled votes during this period was invariably above 10 percent of the total and on some occasions (such as 1974) over 20 percent. In 1992 the annulled vote stood at 3.6 percent. (See also table 2.3.)

TABLE 2.1
GUBERNATORIAL ELECTION RESULTS FOR BAJA CALIFORNIA SINCE 1953

Year	Candidate	Party	# Votes	% Votes
1953	Braulio Maldonado	PRI	60,006	93
	Francisco Cañedo		4,864	8
			64,870	
1959	Eligio Esquivel Méndez	PRI	89,558	66
	Salvador Rosas Magallón	PAN	46,570	34
			136,128	
1965	Raúl Sánchez Díaz	PRI	102,719	73
	Norberto Corella Gil	PAN	37,373	27
			140,092	
1971	Milton Castellanos E.	PRI	148,495	64
	Salvador Rosas Magallón	PAN	82,291	36
			230,786	
1977	Roberto De Lamadrid	PRI	181,760	65
	Héctor Terán Terán	PAN	89,574	32
	Pánfilo Orozco	PPS	5,641	2
	Blas Manrique	PCM	2,169	0.8
			279,144	
1983	Xicoténcatl Leyva	PRI	268,929	66
	Héctor Terán Terán	PAN	121,818	30
	José Luis Alonso	PDM-PSUM	10,215	2.5
	Sergio Quiroz M.	PPS	5,510	1.4
	Roberto Mota Fabela	PRT	2,235	0.6
			408,707	
1989	Ernesto Ruffo Appel	PAN	204,120	52
	Margarita Ortega	PRI	162,294	42
	Martha Maldonado	PRD-PARM	13,017	3.3
	Sergio Quiroz	PPS-PFCRN	9,980	2.5
			389,411	

Source: A. Valderrábano, *Historias del poder: el caso de Baja California* (Mexico City: Grijalbo, 1989).

government, although the party's margin of victory was reduced by some 9 percent from its 1986 level. Only in Mexicali did the PRI retain a solid margin of victory, although here, too, the PAN increased its share of the vote.

By comparing results from congressional races in Baja California over the last three elections (1986, 1989, and 1992), we can construct an image of the spatial distribution of the vote (see table 2.3). These results confirm that support for the PAN tends to be strongest in the urban districts of Tijuana and Ensenada, whereas the PRI is strongest in the rural districts of Mexicali and Ensenada and, to a lesser extent, in

Table 2.2
PRI and PAN Vote in Municipal Elections, 1986–1992

Municipio	Year	Total Votes	PRI	% PRI	PAN	% PAN	Participation Rate (%)
Ensenada	1986	63,690	17,032	27	33,229	52	51
	1989	71,066	24,906	35	36,318	51	53
	1992	95,847	38,733	40	46,373	48	77
Mexicali	1986	204,199	85,000	42	58,780	29	59
	1989	181,533	91,109	50	64,911	36	52
	1992	240,415	144,017	47	103,155	43	82
Tecate	1986	12,116	6,151	51	3,216	27	51
	1989	13,855	6,290	45	6,258	45	47
	1992	21,341	9,194	43	9,700	46	83
Tijuana	1986	175,765	80,255	46	33,083	19	54
	1989	175,917	55,930	32	79,522	45	48
	1992	287,713	126,918	44	133,672	47	80

Sources: Tonatiuh Guillén López, *Baja California: alternancia política y transición democrática* (Tijuana, B.C.: El Colegio de la Frontera Norte/Centro de Investigaciones Interdisciplinarias en Humanidades, Universidad Nacional Autónoma de México, 1993); Comisión Estatal Electoral, "Resultados electorales estatales y muncipalès, *Boletín Estatal* (Gobierno del Estado de Baja California), August 31, 1992, p. 25.

Tecate. This analysis also shows a general trend toward a narrowing in the margins of victory over the six-year period. It is in Mexicali's urban districts (the 1st, 2nd, and 3rd) that one observes some of the tightest races in the state, with margins of victory in the 2 to 9 percent range. These trends seem fairly stable over the three sets of elections. In contrast, the 1986 and 1989 elections in Mexicali's three rural districts (the 4th, 5th, and 6th) appear to be the least competitive statewide, with the PRI's margins of victory in the 22 to 54 percent range. This confirms national polling data, which suggest that the PRI maintains its strongest electoral bases in rural areas (Medina 1991: 12). Nonetheless, it is notable that in the 1992 election the PAN did manage to narrow the gap, considerably reducing the PRI margin of victory in these same rural districts (see table 2.3).

In Tijuana's six congressional districts we see some of the most dramatic reversals of fortune (in both directions) over the six-year period. Moreover, voter preferences in this, the most populous municipality, also appear to be the most volatile. In the 1986 elections the PRI won all six districts with commanding margins of victory, ranging from a low of 24 percent to a high of 35 percent. In 1989 the difference between the two parties remained wide, yet this time the PAN was on the winning end. In the 1992 elections the results showed the two parties to be in close competition, with margins of victory lower than 3 percent

TABLE 2.3
VOTES BY PARTY IN STATE CONGRESSIONAL ELECTIONS, 1986–1992

District	Year	Participation Rate (%)	PRI (%)	PAN (%)	Others (%)	Annulled (%)
1 (Urban Mexicali)	1986	52	45	37	0	8
	1989	51	45	36	5	13
	1992	79	48	43	4	5
2 (Urban Mexicali)	1986	45	37	33	0	25
	1989	51	43	45	6	8
	1992	78	48	44	6	3
3 (Urban Mexicali)	1986	65	42	31	0	22
	1989	50	44	46	6	4
	1992	81	42	48	5	4
4 (Rural Mexicali)	1986	66	48	24	0	23
	1989	57	49	27	8	16
	1992	83	49	39	6	4
5 (Rural Mexicali)	1986	53	58	23	0	14
	1989	45	60	23	13	5
	1992	82	48	43	4	5
6 (Rural Mexicali)	1986	61	72	18	0	4
	1989	51	61	24	10	6
	1992	79	51	39	6	4
7 (Tecate)	1986	51	50	26	0	6
	1989	46	47	46	7	0
	1992	83	45	40	11	3
8 (Tijuana)	1986	47	56	24	0	7
	1989	53	28	41	6	25
	1992	81	46	47	4	3
9 (Tijuana)	1986	58	43	19	0	28
	1989	43	34	54	7	5
	1992	80	45	48	4	3
10 (Tijuana)	1986	52	45	21	0	23
	1989	45	32	51	5	13
	1992	81	46	47	4	3
11 (Tijuana)	1986	47	52	24	0	10
	1989	40	32	62	6	0
	1992	81	38	54	5	3
12 (Tijuana)	1986	50	53	20	0	15
	1989	40	36	53	7	4
	1992	81	45	47	5	3
13 (Tijuana)	1986	48	52	17	0	13
	1989	35	37	47	16	0
	1992	78	42.8	43.3	10	4
14 (Urban Ensenada)	1986	60	26	45	0	17
	1989	53	36	58	6	0
	1992	78	38	51	8	3
15 (Rural Ensenada)	1986	46	58	27	0	5
	1989	43	55	28	13	4
	1992	72	57	31	8	4

Sources: Tonatiuh Guillén López, *Baja California: alternancia política y transición democrática* (Tijuana, B.C.: El Colegio de la Frontera Norte/Centro de Investigaciones Interdisciplinarias en Humanidades, Universidad Nacional Autónoma de México, 1993); Comisión Estatal Electoral, "Resultados electorales estatales y municipales, *Boletín Estatal* (Gobierno del Estado de Baja California), August 31, 1992, p. 25.

in all but one district (Tijuana's 11th district, where the PAN won with a more commanding 16 percent).

In a similar vein, electoral competition also appears to be heating up in Tecate. From the election of 1986 to the one in 1989, the PAN closed the PRI's margin of victory from 24 percent to a razor-close 1 percent. In the 1992 election, which saw the municipal government turned over to the PAN's control, the PRI was able to win the congressional race by a slightly more comfortable 5 percent margin. In Ensenada during the 1986–1992 period, the PAN continued to win the seat in the more urban 14th district by a fairly commanding margin. However, the PRI's percentage of the vote has inched up over the three elections, from 26 percent to 36 percent to 38 percent. In Ensenada's more rural 15th district, the PRI has maintained firm control with 58 percent, 55 percent, and 57 percent of the vote totals, respectively (see table 2.3).

We were especially interested in the 1991 (federal) and 1992 (municipal and state congressional) elections in Baja California because, for the first time, the public had the opportunity to register approval or disapproval of the first three years of PANista governments, especially considering that Ruffo was only then midway through his term. Overall, the results appear to be fairly supportive of the experiences of these opposition governments. In the 1991 federal elections, where the PRI did well nationally (see Colosio 1993), the PAN and the PRI shared equally the six federal deputy seats. Following the spatial pattern identified above, the PAN took all three seats for Tijuana, while the PRI took both Mexicali seats and the 3rd district (Ensenada and Tecate). Statewide, across the six federal electoral districts the PRI won by a marginal plurality (45.85 percent versus 44.68 percent). In the 1992 state elections, although the PAN lost one of its nine congressional seats, in the 2nd (urban) district in Mexicali, the party did win the municipal presidency in Tecate. This has given the PAN control over three of Baja California's four city governments (*ayuntamientos*), leaving Mexicali in the PRI camp.

Aside from the PAN's ability to hold on to its 1989 gains, two additional points regarding the 1992 vote are important. First was the ability of the PRI to make a significant comeback in Tijuana. As noted earlier, in the 1989 municipal and congressional elections in Tijuana the PAN was able to dramatically reverse past trends. In 1989 it won the municipality for the first time and by a fairly comfortable margin. However, in the 1992 vote for municipal president, the PAN's margin of victory slipped to a narrow 3 percent (table 2.3). A similar narrowing of the margins was seen in all races for Tijuana's six congressional districts (table 2.3). This narrowing of the PAN's support was most likely due to the public's negative response toward the widely publicized internecine conflict among competing PANista factions within the elected membership of the municipal council (*cabildo*), which had caused the consequent disruption of Tijuana's municipal government (points to which we return in chapter 4). Second was the impact of the 1992 state electoral reform on voter turnout—which we discuss in more detail below.

Also, we now have the 1994 federal election results available to us, and in Baja California (as elsewhere in its traditional strongholds) the PAN lost considerable ground to the PRI. Indeed, the PRI opened up a ten-point advantage, and the PAN lost the three (of six) federal congressional districts that it had held previously. Nor did the PAN win the senatorial race. The imminence of the 1995 gubernatorial and local congressional races makes these results particularly interesting—and not a little worrying for the PAN. We are not sure whether this represents a "punishment vote" against the Ruffo government, or whether Mexican populations may be differentiating between the way in which they vote for federal government and the way in which they vote for state and city hall government. We believe that it is desirable and important to differentiate between the campaign discourse of national versus local elections, but we also doubt whether that difference can explain a margin as large as 10 percent. Prior to the 1994 economic crisis and the PAN's victory in Jalisco in early 1995, the 1994 results did not auger well for the PAN's election hopes in summer 1995.

Electoral Reform and the 1992 Elections

Electoral reform was an important issue in the 1992 election: that contest provided the first test of one of the Ruffo administration's principal objectives upon taking office in 1989. Ruffo's original reform proposal contained four main objectives: (1) restructuring the State Electoral Commission (CEE); (2) rewriting the rules covering party campaign financing; (3) revising the state's register of voters; and (4) providing all citizens with photo identification cards for voting (known as the credentialization program). Ruffo had been able to accomplish all but the first of these objectives prior to the 1992 election.[6] However, his efforts to construct a State Electoral Commission that would be recognized as impartial by all parties proved to be one of the most contentious issues to come before the 1989–1992 state legislature, and the electoral law that was finally passed in February 1992 did not change the rules by which the CEE's organizational structure would be determined. This meant that for the August 1992 elections, the composition of the CEE was still governed by legal provisions passed under a PRI-dominated congress and state government. The old formula for filling the available positions on the State Electoral Commission gave the advantage to the party in

---

[6]Theoretically, many of these reforms could not be undertaken independently without federal approval, and changes to the register of voters and photo identification cards are supposed to be the responsibility of the Federal Registry (Registro Federal Electoral). However, Ruffo jumped ahead with these reforms and got away with it—at least on the last two counts.

power—now the PAN. It is somewhat ironic that the PRI (which had initially drawn up these rules) now criticized the PAN for "stacking the commission in its favor" (interview with Martina Montenegro, January 1993).

Of much greater significance for the 1992 vote were revisions to the register of voters (the *padrón*) and the credentialization program, which for the first time gave a state government the authority to revise and develop its own electoral rolls and to provide voters with photo identification cards designed to reduce the possibilities for electoral fraud, thereby raising confidence in the electoral process. The credentialization program increased the number of voters on the voter rolls (*lista nominal*) from 759,969 in 1991 to 822,151 in 1992—an increase of 62,182 eligible voters (CEE 1992). This highly publicized program both stirred awareness of the electoral process and helped mobilize voters; its impact upon the participation rates for the August 2, 1992, elections is notable. Looking at participation rates generally over the 1986 to 1992 period, turnout in municipal elections has risen from around 50–54 percent in 1986 and 1989 to a very high 81 percent in 1992 (table 2.3). The credentialization program accounts for part of this increase, but it seems probable also that heightened electoral awareness stemming from the dramatic 1989 wins had a significant effect upon increased levels of voter turnout. One should not, perhaps, expect such a high participation rate in future elections.

In short, therefore, our analysis of electoral results from recent elections in Baja California paints a picture of an electoral arena characterized by increased levels of competition between the two main parties and, in the case of Tecate at least, by *alternancia* of parties in power. This increased competition is the first sign suggestive of democratization in the state's political system. In other chapters we will gauge how far other evidence confirms or contradicts our initial premise of a democratization process that is in train. However, before proceeding, there are other measures by which we may better evaluate whether these election results are leading to a more firm basis of democracy in practice.

Elections, the Composition of Congress, and Governability

The first instance of electoral trends impacting upon governability is found in the legislative realm. Here the departure from a hitherto unquestioned norm of PRI dominance is manifest in a divided congress and often in opposition dominance of a municipal council. Furthermore, the behavior of representatives-at-large may narrow the advantage held by the PRI or the PAN in the state legislature and, to a lesser extent, in the various municipal councils. Such state- and municipal-level processes reflect both the specifics of local and regional political trends and statewide arrangements stipulated by each congress. In turn, this arrangement has been shaped by nationally prescribed formulas for proportional representation at the state and municipal levels. But before we discuss the latter, we should briefly analyze the national context.

National Legislative Precedents

Some level of proportional representation in the federal Congress was established by national-level reforms beginning in the early 1960s. Over the years opposition parties had fared poorly in competition for single-member-district seats, and President Adolfo López Mateos (1958–1964) initiated amendments to Article 54 of the federal constitution in order to facilitate quasi-proportional representation of opposition parties in the national Congress. Technically, the 1963 reforms allowed for the representation of parties obtaining a minimum of 2.5 percent of the national vote. Five congressional seats were to be assigned for the first 2.5 percent of the national vote obtained, with an additional seat awarded for every additional half-percent of the vote gained.

In spite of the potential boost to opposition representation, the twenty-seat cap placed on opposition parties' presence in the national Congress demonstrates the limited nature of this arrangement. In fact, the government also gave seats to both the Authentic Party of the Mexican Revolution (PARM) and the Socialist Popular Party (PPS) (parties closely associated with the PRI) throughout the late 1960s, even though neither party obtained the required 2.5 percent of the national vote. This effectively inflated the congressional representation of these parties vis-à-vis their electoral proportions and led to a (constitutionally) anomalous sub-proportionality for the PRI from 1964 to 1970 (see Baer 1990; Favela 1992; Molinar Horcasitas 1987; Klesner 1991). The constrained nature of the reforms was especially apparent in their impact on the PAN, which increased its national vote to 11.5 percent in 1964, 12.4 percent in 1967, and 13.9 percent in 1970; yet the twenty-seat cap on any non-PRI party in effect kept its representation within the Chamber of Deputies to below 10 percent—at least until 1973 (Mabry 1974).

One result of the 1960s reforms was that they distorted the meaning of electoral competition, especially for the PAN, which had little to gain from a strategy aimed at *local* electoral victories. This distortion is also seen in the inflated, albeit minimal, weight of the PPS and the PARM within the national legislature, as well as in the provision of seats to these parties despite their coming up short of the prescribed minimum percentage. Political power in Mexico remained highly discretionary, rather than constitutionally provided for (Mabry 1974; Bath 1989; González Casanova 1970).

The growing political pressures in Mexico during the late 1960s and early 1970s led to a new round of reforms in 1972 and, more importantly, in 1977. The first round lowered the total vote threshold for a presence in the Congress from 2.5 percent to 1.5 percent, and the twenty-seat cap for opposition parties was raised to twenty-five seats. These reforms had the effect of extending constitutional legality to the seats held by the PPS and the PARM, but they did not end either the overrepresentation of these small parties or the underrepresentation of the PAN (Mabry 1974). Indeed, while increasing the raw numbers of opposition representatives in the legislature, the sum impact was a return to inflated proportions for the PRI at a time when its weight in the national vote was decreasing. The 1977 reform went much further. It provided for a de facto increase in the opposition's representation to 25 percent of the national legislature (one hundred of the then four hundred seats). These at-large seats were to be distributed on the basis of proportional representation to the qualifying minority parties.[7] The remaining 75 percent of the congressional seats would be determined on the basis of the official electoral returns from the single-member districts— the *uninominal* seats. A second outcome of the 1977 reform was to facilitate the formation of new (but small) parties at the regional or national level, thus potentially fragmenting the political opposition further.

An additional round of reforms in 1986 raised the opposition representation yet again, to a *minimum* 30 percent of the now enlarged legislature (comprising 500 seats), but with the potential for even greater opposition gains. Now up to 40 percent of the at-large seats were available to the opposition (i.e., 200 of the 500 seats). Importantly, however, the PRI virtually guaranteed its own hold on the legislature by extending at-large seats to *any* party receiving less than 50 percent of the legislative seats, thereby ensuring that the party with the largest plurality had sufficient seats to obtain a majority position in the lower house under this, the "governability clause."

Significantly, by 1989 opposition parties had acquired close to 50 percent of the seats in the Chamber of Deputies, thus suggesting the first true alteration in the PRI's power within this house of Congress. With PRI dominance there dropping to a baseline majority, well below the 66 percent majority required for constitutional changes, the PRI had to seek coalition partners for the purposes of amending the constitution. This is important in light of the fact that Mexican presidents regularly initiate constitutional amendments through the legislative process and that President Salinas's neoliberal policies required the revision of several constitutional pillars closely associated with revolutionary ideals. The imperative that the PRI enter into coalition building lessened somewhat following that party's

---

[7]Qualifications aimed to exclude the smallest national parties, as was the case under the 1972 reforms, while any party winning sixty or more seats through single-member-district elections could not receive any at-large seats.

the party line. Indeed, quite the opposite: he frequently voted with the PRI and as a consequence was expelled from his own party shortly after entering office. Thus, both the PARM and PRD members held their seats not as party representatives but as virtual independents.

The double irony is that at-large seats are technically designed for the purpose of representing opposition parties. Instead, these cases reveal two instances of privatized representation—by which we mean the individualized exercise of a public office without reference to a party or other public agent—amounting to more than 10 percent of the 1989–1992 legislature and wielding considerable leverage vis-à-vis the major parties. Having effectively lost one of its own party members and on shaky terms with its two most probable allies, where could the PAN contingent turn for additional votes? The two remaining at-large seats, those of the PPS and the PFCRN, were held by longtime PRI allies, if not PRI "satellites." These representatives frequently joined with the PRI, leaving the PAN contingent with a very precarious plurality indeed.

The first experiences of this supposedly PAN-dominated congress, consequently, were of a truly contentious arena of debate and power jockeying. The congress successfully blocked a number of Governor Ruffo's initiatives, most notably on electoral reform, although the PRI was also unable to carry out its own agenda. The final outcome was a compromise of sorts—perhaps a congressional first when compared with the assured passage of PRI governors' legislation in the past. The PRI eventually acceded to PANista proposals for an independent electoral commission but succeeded in toning down some of Governor Ruffo's proposals.[9]

In short, during the 1989–1992 session, both major parties appear to have been caught off guard. For the PRI, finding itself in a minority position was an unpleasant novelty; it might have fared better had it ensured a more competent congressional contingent. PRI minority leader Martina Montenegro (the PRI's youngest and only female representative) often received only limited support from other PRI representatives. The PRI appears to have suffered from the old-style politics of selecting congressional candidates according to internal party considerations, specifically the need to balance out representation of its worker, peasant, and popular sectors, rather than focusing on voter appeal and "electability." Nor was the PAN much more successful in its choice of candidates and leaders, as seen in the defection of Representative Dolores de Méndez.

Turning briefly to the 1992–1995 legislature, we find an even closer competition between the PAN and the PRI. Due to a reversal in Mexicali's 2nd district, the PAN lost one seat to the PRI and entered with a

---

[9]The PRI delegates wanted the commission to be composed of the outgoing congress representatives, who alone would approve or disapprove of the incoming group of representatives. Interview with Martina Montenegro, January 1993.

marginal plurality of eight to seven. When we factor in that the PRD, with a mere 3.3 percent of the popular vote, was awarded all four of the at-large seats, the congressional dynamic promised to be markedly different. These seats gave the PRD more than one-fifth (21 percent) of the congressional vote. And while an optimistic reading of this situation would see a shift to the PAN's advantage, the initial experience was one of the PRD bloc holding together for maximum leverage vis-à-vis both the PAN and the PRI.

In our view this "construction" of pluralities in state congresses, while perhaps well intentioned, generates major anomalies of questionable authenticity. Clearly it is an unusual situation when a small minority vote multiplies into such a significant congressional force. The irony is that if we recall the origins of Mexico's proportional representative arrangements, we see a system change that has now come full circle. Initially the idea was to give small opposition parties a limited voice in the national legislature, while the governability clause ensured an overall majority for the principal party. The potential consequences of extending these arrangements to the state and municipal levels were never really thought through, probably because the very possibility of PRI losses was rarely considered. Here we encounter the unexpected. Not only has the PRI fallen from the ruling heights, but a party with minimal electoral support in 1992 (the PRD) has acquired a vote of disproportionate substance, raising real questions of governability for those elected and mandated to govern. Perhaps as the PAN's former congressional president suggested, it is time to reconfigure the at-large system (interview with Bernardo Borbón Vílchez, January 11, 1993). At a minimum, the new congress promises to test, again, the limits of authority of an institution which has traditionally been subservient to the state and federal executives.

Conclusion: Democratization and Electoral Pluralism

In Baja California, both the PRI and the PAN are changing the way in which they relate to the electorate. Previously the PRI was able to rely upon support from its three corporatist organizations to ensure electoral victory, but now it must look for new bases of support if it is to remain a viable party in the state. In Guillén López's words, "this is the first PRI that must really function as a political party" (*Proceso*, September 9, 1991). Moreover, a new style of management and government has begun to emerge which relies far less upon the patronage and clientelism of yesteryear—which had suited the PRI's purposes so well (Ward 1986; Bailey 1988). The PAN, too, finds itself planning a new role. Once the perennial opposition party, it currently controls the governments of Tijuana, Ensenada, and Tecate, as well as that of Baja California State. It is seeking to rid itself of its "party of the elite" label. While not yet ready to become the "party of the people," it seems at least to be moving in that direction. Furthermore, the PAN must make the transition from opposition party to governing party proper or it risks displacement in future elections.

Fundamentally, the transition from one-party rule to pluralism in the state will involve reconstructing the basic rules of the political game. As Adam Przeworski has pointed out, this process involves reformulating "(a) the criteria for being admitted as a political participant, (b) the courses of action that constitute admissible strategies, and (c) the criteria by which conflicts are terminated" (Przeworski 1986: 56). For the PRI, these changes inevitably mean that the party will have to exist in an environment where political outcomes are not certain. Accepting uncertainty about who will exercise political power, who will control political resources, and what policy agendas will be pursued—conditions basic to multiparty democracy—will require the development of a political culture with a high degree of trust in political institutions and their ability to produce compromise (Przeworski 1986: 59).

In the past, of course, competition has existed only *within* the PRI, such that once uncertainty was settled through the president's personal designation of his successor, the expectancy was for a closing of the ranks, on the understanding that any existing imbalances would be redressed in the future (Smith 1979; Purcell and Purcell 1980). Since the mid-1980s, there has been growing uncertainty within the PRI as to whether these rules still apply, particularly regarding the redress of imbalances from one administration to the next. Thus, whether through internal party reform or through the experience of having been the party in opposition (as in Baja California), the PRI must begin to look to the political institutions themselves for opportunities to contest, win, and exercise power in the future. The PAN, too, must be prepared to let go of those levels of government it may lose in future elections and, along with the PRI, place its faith in political institutions. Thus far, *alternancia* has been unidirectional. Although it is too early to discern the level of institutionalization of this fundamental aspect of the democratic process, we are confident that the process has begun and is firmly established. Nevertheless, the future remains precarious. The acid test will come in the response of the PRI if—and when—it wins back power at the local and state levels.

3

Political Recruitment, Government, and Partisanship

Introduction: Democratization through Government

As we have seen in the preceding chapter on election results, electoral competition has increased significantly in Baja California, and the emergence of multiparty government (in the legislature) has led to significant changes in the way the state is governed. In this chapter our concern is to assess whether these changes are also suggestive of greater democracy and openness insofar as official recruitment, governance, and the formulation and implementation of policy agendas are concerned. In the area of recruitment, we will see that the emphasis on competence and administrative efficiency that we find in the PAN municipal governments in Tijuana and Ensenada is also becoming apparent in the recruitment of PRI officials in Mexicali. The provision of services at state and municipal levels is marked by greater transparency and less corruption. And while PANista administrations are breaking traditional PRI corporatist structures, the PRI, too, is exhibiting signs of a more rational and streamlined approach to urban governance. Finally, partisanship at a municipal level appears to have been reduced, although it continues at the state level in an effort to compete with federal programs. The leitmotif running through Baja California today is one of greater efficiency and competence in governance. In this chapter we propose to evaluate how far, and in what ways, government practice has become more efficient and honest.

Recruitment to Government Office: Better Officials, Better Government?

In looking at the social origins and orientation of a sample of elected PRI and PAN leaders, primarily in the legislative arena, Roderic Camp (1995: 79) argues that "at the moment the PRI represents the dominant middle-class view, while the PAN represents another, minority sector of the middle class. Thus, the PAN adds to political diversity *within* the middle classes who control Mexican leadership, but not diversity *among* classes." As one might expect, Camp found a somewhat higher association with the private sector among PANista officials. "For example, 14 percent of PANista leaders held business management posts prior to their first national political office compared to only 5 percent of all establishment government officials" (1995: 73). In addition, while PANista leaders, like those from other parties, tend to be better educated than the general populace, they exhibit a greater reliance on private educational institutions at the primary and secondary level. Also, while PAN leaders attend the National University of Mexico (UNAM) at about the same rate as their PRI counterparts, they show a greater interest in business administration and eschew economics, a field prominent among PRI leaders (Camp 1995: 73).[1]

In our earlier work (Rodríguez and Ward 1992) we proposed a three-fold typology of PANista city officials. Specifically, we identified: (a) longtime party members, (b) prospective career politicians, and (c) appointees from the private sector. In Chihuahua we found that the first two groups were numerically fairly small, that the largest group comprised officials drawn from the private sector, and that most of these officials, perforce, returned to that sector in 1986 once the PANistas failed to get reelected. In Baja California we observed a similar provenance for PAN politicians and government officials, but here they appear to settle into one of three possible career trajectories: (a) an elected office track, (b) an appointed office track, and (c) a civic duty track.

The Elected Office Career Track

For the first time ever, in 1989 the PAN was challenged to recruit candidates for elected and appointed government positions at both the municipal and state levels. Although the PAN had only five hundred members statewide, it was nevertheless able to win the governorship, nine seats in the state congress, and, in both Tijuana and Ensenada, the municipal presidency and a majority on the city council. Because of this unprecedented success, the PAN had to fill a large number of positions and, inevitably, had to look beyond the core of longtime party militants. It appears from our data that those who are attracted to elected positions show a higher (prior) commitment to the PAN than do those serving in the other two tracks. The most obvious example of an individual in the elected office track is Salvador Rosas Magallón, who ran for state governor in 1959 and again in 1971, and no fewer than four times was among the PAN's front-runner candidates for the office of federal president (interview with Rosas Magallón, January 14,

---

[1] Camp's results regarding the PAN are based on a survey of 101 PANista leaders who have held, almost exclusively, legislative positions at the state or national level. It is likely that many of these differences would be even more sharply pronounced had Camp also included a larger number of appointed PANista officials at the state and municipal levels.

1993). Other examples include Héctor Terán Terán, the federal senator for Baja California; Bernardo Borbón Vílchez, the leader of the PAN bloc in the state congress (1989–1992) who previously ran for office on a PAN slate; and René Núñez Higuera, a deputy in the state congress who served as the local leader of the PAN in Ensenada. Javier Moctezuma y Coronado, another PAN deputy in the state congress, had been president of the PAN municipal committee in Tijuana and a federal deputy for the PAN in the 52nd legislature.

But most recently, and particularly from 1989 onward, the PAN appears to have modified somewhat its criteria for selecting candidates. Instead of running candidates who exemplify strong party commitment, the PAN now concentrates on selecting individuals who are electable. Electability, not party commitment, is the driving criterion. For example, Ernesto Ruffo Appel, who joined the PAN in 1985, was the party's candidate for municipal president in Ensenada the very next year. In another instance, the PAN entreated Jesús del Palacio Lafontaine to contend for the municipal presidency of Ensenada in 1989 when Oscar Sánchez del Palacio could not run, yet del Palacio Lafontaine only became a PAN member a short time before he *left* that office in 1992. Moreover, neither of the PAN federal deputies for Baja California was a member of the party at the time of the 1990 elections. And Carlos Montejo Favela, who was elected municipal president of Tijuana in 1989, had to be lobbied extensively before agreeing to run; he joined the PAN just ten minutes before registering his candidacy. Thus not all PANistas in the elected office track are longtime members of the PAN.

From our analysis of the 1989 data, it appears that there were two subtracks with regard to elected office. The first was a legislative subtrack and covered deputies in the state congress and municipal council members (*regidores*). The second subtrack covered elected executive branch positions—the state governorship and municipal presidencies. Those who sought election to legislative positions in 1989 tended to have a longer and closer association with the PAN, while those seeking executive branch offices (a very small sample of three) tended to have weaker party identification. This might suggest that party affiliation is an important criterion for legislative positions, while administrative competence is more determinant for executive positions.[2] However, our data on the 1992

---

[2] We should note here that a similar trend may be observed for the PRI at state and national levels. Elected legislative positions tend to fall to career party militants and politicians rewarded for their loyalty and work on behalf of the party, while noncareer PRIístas dominate in the executive branch, governorships, secretaryships, etc., and are appointed and/or elected for their competence and loyalty to the national leadership. Elsewhere (Rodríguez and Ward 1994b) we have analyzed this apparent separation of career tracks, but we have also noted a marked blurring in recent years as the PRI recognizes that it needs to incorporate a more technocratic and electable cadre into legislative and municipal government, individuals like PRI municipal president Milton Castellanos Gout (Mexicali, 1989–1992).

elections, while based upon another extremely small sample (two of the three municipal presidents), contradict the results observed in 1989. In 1992, Oscar Sánchez del Palacio (an Ensenada council member from 1986 to 1989) and Héctor Osuna Jaime (a party member since 1983 and a PAN deputy in the 1989–1992 state congress) won the municipal presidencies of Ensenada and Tijuana, respectively.

Given the constitutional law barring Mexican politicians from seeking reelection to the same office and the small size of the PAN in Baja California, perhaps one should not be surprised to find officials crossing from one subtrack to another, especially since this was one of the first cases in which a PANista government had extended beyond three years. As one might suspect, the 1992 data suggest that, when it can, the PAN prefers to draft candidates who are committed to the party and who demonstrate a strong propensity for good governance once they are elected.

While our biographical data on candidates elected in 1992 are not as comprehensive as those for 1989, we observed that the trend of nominating individuals with a fairly strong party identification for legislative branch offices seems to continue. For example, four out of nine members in the current Tijuana city council joined the PAN before 1989 (interview with Héctor Osuna, January 11, 1993). César Mancillas Hernández, a deputy in the current state congress, was a council member in Ensenada from 1986 to 1989 and an alternate for senator in 1988. Rafaela Martínez Cantú, another deputy in the 1992 state congress, was an alternate for the 1989–1992 congress. Unlike earlier years, where we found several key candidates who were not even members of the party, in 1992 we did not find a single candidate who was not a member of the PAN. As the PAN's governing experience has grown, so too has the number of candidates with party membership.

Name recognition also seems to be a factor in PAN recruitment. Ernesto Ruffo, for example, was a prominent Ensenada businessman when he ran for municipal president in 1986. Three years later he had acquired a high profile and a statewide reputation, in part because of then governor Xicoténcatl Leyva's hostility toward Ruffo's municipal government in Ensenada. Other PANistas with strong name recognition were Héctor Terán Terán, a federal senator and longtime and well-known PAN political figure; Jorge Esparza, a PAN federal deputy and former radio announcer widely popular in Baja California; Jesús del Palacio Lafontaine and Carlos Montejo Favela, prominent businessmen in Ensenada and Tijuana, respectively; and Oscar Sánchez del Palacio, who was well known in Ensenada when he ran for municipal president in 1992.

Electability seems to be a continuing criterion for the PAN, as the interesting case of Héctor Osuna Jaime (the current municipal president of Tijuana) demonstrates. Osuna did not win the majority of votes at the PAN's nominating convention in Tijuana, which is the requirement for becoming the PAN's candidate to the municipal presidency, and under party rules the selection was referred to the state committee. Even though Osuna had placed third at the nominating convention, he received strong support among the members of the state committee and was given the nomination.[3] What likely accounts for Osuna's selection is the fact that he had run successfully for state deputy from Tijuana in 1989. Since it appeared that the municipal presidency race in Tijuana would be close (the PRI was running a popular local candidate and cousin of President Salinas), Osuna's proven ability to win election in Tijuana made him the choice of the PAN. Thus, unlike the PRI in previous years, the PAN clearly weighs a potential candidate's local popularity when determining who to run. However, as the Osuna example also illustrates, the definition of electability may go beyond an individual's popularity with the party faithful.[4]

It seems probable, too, that alignment with Ruffo and the absence of any association with the dissident wing of the PAN are important criteria in the selection of candidates for government office. Ruffo appears to have blocked Salvador Rosas Magallón's 1991 bid for a seat in the federal Senate. At the last minute (indeed, some argued that the closing date had passed), Governor Ruffo had then government secretary and party heavyweight Héctor Terán Terán declare himself a candidate. Terán was selected and ultimately won the election, but not before Rosas Magallón accused him of "irresponsibility and disloyalty." In turn, Rosas Magallón was denounced for washing the party's dirty linen in public.[5] Other cases include Héctor Osuna's selection by the state committee, despite his not being chosen at the nominating convention, and Oscar Sánchez del Palacio, who left his position as Ensenada's secretary of budget and planning in order to run for the municipal presidency. Prima facie, at least, it appears that Ruffo is trying to keep his people in, or—more accurately—the old guard out.

Winning an election is one thing, but governing is something quite different. While the individuals we interviewed from the PRI and the PRD were, as expected, critical of Governor Ruffo's performance, and while Carlos Montejo Favela clearly had problems dealing with city council members when he was municipal president of Tijuana, by and large PAN elected executive officials do seem able to hold their own. The situation is somewhat different for legislative branch officials because

---

[3] According to a report in *El Mexicano*, Héctor Terán Terán, Eugenio Elorduy Walther, and Bernardo Borbón Vílchez (all longtime party militants) were among the selecting officials who supported Osuna.

[4] One obvious shortcoming in these data (as with Camp's data, cited earlier) is that invariably the biographies are of successful candidates, and we have precious little information about the PRI and PAN candidates who failed to win office.

[5] Guillén López (1993: 116) interprets Ruffo's determined stance against Rosas Magallón as an attempt to ensure that the latter did not take the debate and his own personal complaints into the national forum of the Senate.

this branch has historically been subsidiary to the executive. As the legislative branch struggles to recover lost powers, the quality of legislative branch personnel comes to be of singular importance. In this regard, Bernardo Borbón Vílchez regretted that some of his former colleagues in the 1989–1992 state congress were not better qualified. Borbón Vílchez was referring to all deputies and was clearly including some belonging to the PAN. He went on to express similar concerns about the deputies in the current congress (interview with Borbón Vílchez, January 11, 1993). Although Martina Montenegro, leader of the PRI bloc in the 1989–1992 state congress, took issue with Borbón Vílchez's perspective, she nevertheless agreed that the performance of some of the elderly deputies in the congress was less than competent (interview with Montenegro, January 13, 1993). Governor Ruffo also observed that the deputies in the state congress tended to be overly partisan: "they are party members first and deputies afterward." He, too, was critical of their inexperience in governance and, in some cases, their lack of formal education. In his view, deputies "tend to be very good in dealing with people, going into neighborhoods, etc., but when they start seeing themselves in the newspaper they don't quite know how to react, and they become overly preoccupied with image" (interview with Ruffo, March 12, 1993). In order for the state congress to wrest more power from the executive in the future, all parties must be able to recruit accomplished politicians—candidates who can both win elections and govern effectively once in office. Our observations suggest that thus far all parties, including the PAN, have achieved the former but have yet to achieve the latter.

The Appointed Office Career Track

The first feature of note is that being an active PAN militant did not automatically result in an individual being appointed to a government post. Many observers, including the state head of the PAN, the bishop of Mexicali, and some appointed state officials, remarked that there were a number of longtime PAN members who had expected to be appointed to government posts but were not, causing some tension within the party. This observation is borne out by Governor Ruffo's initial cabinet appointments. Of the twenty-two appointees for whom we have biographical data, none ran on any party slate (either state or municipal) in 1989. This further strengthens our proposition that the criteria for securing elective and appointed office appear to be different and that other factors besides past service to the party are considered when selecting people for appointed office.

Ruffo's initial cabinet appointments also show a heavy reliance on people with private-sector experience. Of the twenty-two appointees, eleven were businessmen (although a couple were longtime and prominent members of the PAN); another two were businessmen with some experience in government (in Ensenada under Ruffo); and only six were experienced government officials, three having served in Ensenada and three in state-level administrative positions during former PRI administrations. Of the remaining three appointees, all were associated with higher education in some fashion. Therefore, our data suggest that appointed PANista officials are more likely than PRI officials to have a business background. While this is consistent with Camp's (1995) findings, we discerned greater differences than did Camp between the PRI and the PAN, largely because our sample includes a greater proportion of persons in executive positions than in legislative ones (see Rodríguez and Ward 1992).

We did not have full educational backgrounds for all twenty-two individuals included in the sample of appointees discussed above. However, among those for whom we were able to gather this information, six were graduates of the Monterrey Technological Institute (ITESM), in addition to Governor Ruffo, who is also an ITESM alumnus. To the extent that Ruffo has a camarilla, it appears to have been formed around the ITESM. Other universities represented were the University of Baja California (two individuals), the University of Guadalajara (two), the Autonomous University of Guadalajara (two), the University of Sonora (two), and the National University of Mexico (one). The leading fields of study were business (five in administration and three in public accounting), law (six), engineering (two), chemistry (two), architecture, medicine, and agriculture. Once again, just as Camp found, there was not a single economist![6] Thus there appears to be a growing trend of differentiation by occupation between PANista leaders and their PRI counterparts.

Another distinctive feature of Ruffo's appointments is that they cross party lines. For example, in Ensenada in 1986 Ruffo had appointed Alfredo Rosales Green as director of public safety and he recommended María de los Angeles Dávalos to be his chief of staff (*oficial mayor*), even though both were members of the PRI.[7] At the state level in 1989, Ruffo again appointed Rosales Green, this time as director of transit and transport. He also appointed PRI party member Eduardo Krauss Coronel as attorney general (although he was later replaced). Thus the PAN appears to have made an attempt to reach out not only to the private sector but also to members of other political parties in order to fill

---

[6]This is not surprising given the traditional left-wing association with economics as a discipline, and with the political economy tradition at the National University of Mexico in particular. For this generation, therefore, there is little likelihood of finding many PANistas with degrees in economics. This will change in time: both the Monterrey Technological Institute (ITESM) and the Autonomous Technological Institute of Mexico (ITAM) have developed well-regarded degree programs in economics (especially microeconomics), and we may expect PANistas (and PRIístas) increasingly to come through that career route.

[7]In the end he selected a PANista as his chief of staff.

appointed positions—a feature we also observed in Chihuahua (Rodríguez and Ward 1992).

In part we suspect that this willingness to include members of other parties in cabinet posts reflects the fact that the PAN has only a small cadre of qualified people upon which to draw, and therefore it is obliged to incorporate experienced personnel from the PRI. How this practice will continue, as the pool of experienced PANistas grows, is less certain. Our interviews with various PANista executive officers suggest that, other things being equal, they would usually choose someone of their own political persuasion; when that was not possible, they would only consider someone who was not an intensely partisan PRIísta. Moreover, since the PRI was split locally, the selection of a PRI sympathizer would not automatically be viewed as a betrayal. There are some positions, too, where it may make good sense to bring a PRI member on board and/or to confirm a senior official from the previous administration in his job, at least in the short term. This is particularly true where deep, long-term changes are required, where resistance to change is likely to be high, and where the potential for criticism and instability is also high—at least during the transition to the new government.[8] Governors Carlos Medina Plascencia and Francisco Barrio—of Guanajuato and Chihuahua, respectively—both appointed PRIístas as their government secretaries. In the case of Medina Plascencia, this was almost certainly an imposition; nevertheless, the appointment might be considered to make strategic good sense since the state government secretary has primary responsibility for interacting with the federal government as well as with the state congress. However, it was not an option chosen by Governor Ruffo.

There were also a number of officials at the cabinet and subcabinet levels who had held several appointed positions consecutively, suggesting, as we found in Chihuahua, that some officials hope to remain in government as long as the PAN continues to win elections (Rodríguez and Ward 1992). For example, Carlos Ahumada Arruti, Héctor Llamas, Isauro López Cárdenas, and Alfredo Rosales Green all held positions on the Ensenada city council under Ruffo. After Ruffo won the Baja California governorship in 1989, all of them agreed to work in his new state-level administration. Another example is Oscar Sánchez del Palacio, who was a council member in Ensenada from 1986 to 1989, moved to Mexicali to serve as secretary of budget and planning in 1989 under Governor Ruffo, and later returned to Ensenada to run (successfully) for the municipal presidency in 1992.

---

[8]In a similar vein, and to the surprise of many, President Salinas appointed an old-guard PRI hard-liner (Gutiérrez Barrios) to be his first government secretary—probably for two reasons: first, to assure the party's old guard that their voices would be heard in the cabinet; and second, to have someone to take the heat when Salinas cracked down on crime and some corrupt union bosses. Although he did not need to cross party lines, Salinas saw the expediency of stepping outside his own group in making that particular appointment.

We also found midterm adjustments occurring in Ruffo's administration. For example, Alfredo Rosales Green, once director of transit and transport, had moved to become director of the Civil Protection Unit. Other examples include Rodolfo Valdez Gutiérrez, who held a series of important government jobs at the state level; Rafael Ayala López who, after resigning as state secretary of education, took up a position as special adviser to the interior minister; and Bernardo Borbón Vílchez, a former deputy in the state congress, who also went to work for the interior minister. Thus, even where individuals are moved around, they rarely exit the administration entirely. The precise significance of this pattern of career shifting can only be determined if the PAN wins the governorship in 1995 and allows the trend to develop further.

The Civic Duty Career Track

In conversations with a number of elected and appointed officials, we found that many of them exhibit low degrees of PAN partisanship and that they were recruited specifically for their current positions, taking the jobs out of a sense of civic duty rather than with the expectation that they would be a springboard to careers in government. For example, the head of the Social Security Institute for State Workers–Baja California (ISSSTECALI) joined the PAN only recently and does not identify with many of the party militants who adhere to the PAN's conservative tenets. Also, many officeholders drawn from the business community indicated their intention to return to the private sector after their terms expire; only time will tell whether these officials follow through with their stated intentions. A case in point is Jesús del Palacio Lafontaine, the former municipal president of Ensenada, who in 1991 asserted at length that he had no political aspirations of any kind and that he intended to limit his political career to three years and then return to his business (*El Mexicano*, February 28, 1991). One year later, he relocated to Mexicali and accepted a senior position in the Ruffo administration as chief cabinet coordinator (*coordinador de gabinetes*). It remains to be seen if del Palacio Lafontaine's experience is the exception or the rule. If PAN officials from the private sector continue in elected or appointed positions instead of returning to their businesses, this would ease the recruiting challenge facing the PAN.

PAN Recruiting: An Overview

The PAN's electoral success has produced positive and negative impacts on the recruiting process. On the one hand, electoral success may attract to the PAN people with political ambitions who previously would not have considered the party to be a sufficiently viable political force to attract their adherence.[9] On the other hand, when the PAN was almost

---

[9] This may account for much of the PAN's recent growth, even though, as noted earlier, merely being a party member is no guarantee of getting a government job.

certain to lose, candidates were willing to offer their names for a slate, confident that their daily lives would not be affected. For example, one Tijuana council member who was elected with Montejo Favela in 1989 observed that she never thought she would win (interview with Concepción López Serrano, January 13, 1993). Now a PAN candidate must be willing both to campaign and to serve in government if elected.

PAN membership statewide increased from 500 to 4,500 between 1989 and 1992, and this growth expanded the pool from which recruiters can select candidates for elective and appointed positions. However, an expanded pool does not mean that PAN leaders will select all officials from within the party. Particularly in the case of the executive branch, where ability to govern may be a more important attribute than party affiliation, PANista leaders have shown a tendency thus far to appoint party outsiders much more frequently than do their PRIísta counterparts. However, there is also widespread agreement with Héctor Osuna, the current municipal president of Tijuana, who has stressed the importance of recruiting officials for appointed positions who are both competent *and* PANistas (interview with Osuna, March 13, 1993). In time, the criteria for PAN appointments to administrative positions may come to resemble more closely those traditionally associated with the PRI.

Filling key positions in the Baja California state government and in three municipal governments surely has been a challenge to the PAN, given the party's low membership statewide. Continued electoral success at the municipal level provides a training ground for PAN officials who may later be tapped for service at the state level. Of Governor Ruffo's initial twenty-two appointments, five had served with him in the Ensenada municipal government from 1986 to 1989. Further, if a significant number of PAN officials do indeed return to their private-sector enterprises once they have completed their terms in office, then future executive officers will have to recruit replacements who are sympathetic to the party and who are also competent officials along the lines emphasized by Héctor Osuna: "Nonmilitants and cross-party appointments do not work." Osuna was adamant that he wanted PANistas or, at the very least, individuals who were not "bound to another ideology." Osuna noted that both Ruffo and Montejo had been hurt by having to appoint PRIístas to important positions, "because they always find the means to block plans and programs" (interview with Osuna, March 13, 1993).

How can the PAN improve its ability to staff the different levels of government with PANista militants? The party could alleviate the shortfall of qualified candidates by significantly expanding its membership base. For the present, the PAN's rigorous membership requirements (including recommendation by a current party member, an in-depth course on PANista principles, a probationary period, etc.) inhibit its ability to become a mass-based party. Its strict entry requirements mean that the PAN will have to mount an intensive recruiting effort if it is to expand its membership significantly.

The PRI Recruitment Process in Mexicali

The preceding paragraphs have discussed PAN recruitment of candidates for office in the state government and in the three municipalities governed by the PAN. This discussion would be incomplete, however, without considering what happens in the one municipality that is not governed by the PAN. This is the case of Mexicali, where the PRI retained control of the municipal presidency in the 1992 elections. By assaying the PRI's recruitment process, we can pinpoint distinctive features in the processes followed by both parties.

Unlike the PAN, the PRI has the benefit of many years of experience at the state and municipal levels. And as a mass-based party with a long tradition, it has no shortage of committed members with significant expertise in politics and government. Name recognition, though perhaps less important than in the past, remains a significant element in some PRI candidacies. Milton Castellanos Gout, the former municipal president of Mexicali, comes from a distinguished family with generations of political experience. His father was a senator and former governor. Castellanos Gout himself was a PRI deputy in the state congress from 1986 to 1989, before being elected municipal president of Mexicali. Another example is Javier Camarena Salinas, the PRI candidate for the Tijuana municipal presidency in 1992 and President Salinas's cousin; he was nominated partly in the hope that name recognition would bring him electoral victory.

Martina Montenegro, the former head of the PRI bloc in the state congress, mentioned that the PRI is making a real effort to bring in young, qualified candidates (interview with Montenegro, January 13, 1993). For example, Javier Camarena Salinas, who is in his mid-thirties, is purportedly intelligent, qualified, and popular among Tijuana voters. Some observers believe that Camarena Salinas's popularity was the key factor accounting for his very strong showing in the 1992 elections in Tijuana, more important than the backlash vote against the PAN following three years of municipal government marked by intraparty bickering. Francisco Pérez Tejada, the 1992 PRI candidate for municipal president in Mexicali, is also well known locally. The PRI now appears to seek candidates who not only have strong PRI credentials but also are popular in, or at least acceptable to, the local community. It will require more time and further study to assess whether these are cosmetic changes, exceptions to the rule, or significant institutional shifts.

In one of our interviews, Castellanos Gout stated that, in government office, competence is of paramount importance. Therefore, he took care to appoint officials who not only had an association with the PRI but also had significant technical qualifications. For example, his director of public safety, Dionisio Hivales Corral, was a longtime PRI member who had also been director and instructor at the police academy and had received training in the United States. The city treasurer, Carlos Topete Noriega, is a public accountant and longtime acquaintance of Castellanos Gout. It does indeed appear that the PRI is emphasizing technical competence when making appointments to office. Young, competent, and locally popular candidates seem to be selected with increasing frequency. Competence and administrative efficiency were certainly hallmarks of the Mexicali municipal government under Castellanos Gout, and several of his senior officials on the 1989–1992 city council were fairly young. In addition, the PRI assigned 28-year-old René Arturo Gómez Michel to direct a statewide effort to spearhead the Urban Popular Territorial Movement (Movimiento Popular Territorial), recently emerged out of the erstwhile National Confederation of Popular Organizations (CNOP, later the National Union for Citizen Linkage [UNE]) as the party's principal spatial organization of the popular sector. It appears that PRI opposition governments and the party itself have modified their recruiting patterns in order to cope with a changing political landscape.

The State-Level Development Agenda and Performance

The evidence we gathered indicates that the PAN's recruitment process has generated cohorts of PANista leaders who perceive and prioritize state and municipal matters differently than do their PRI predecessors or counterparts and who are actively attempting to change the way in which state and municipal agendas are implemented. During Ruffo's election campaign for the governorship, the PAN advocated greater citizen participation (PAN 1989), arguing that individual participation in the electoral process is one of the salient features that distinguishes the PAN from the PRI's philosophy, which traditionally had focused less on individuals and more on its corporatist structures.

Upon taking office, Ruffo had to confront several problems deliberately created by the outgoing administration of interim governor Oscar Baylón. These included a budgetary deficit which left Ruffo unable to pay the end-of-year bonuses traditionally given to state employees (*Novedades*, November 1, 1989, p. 3); a belligerent state employees' union determined to resist any attempts to cut personnel (Guillén López 1993: 89); and two pieces of legislation passed by the PRI-dominated legislature just weeks before Ruffo was sworn in. One sought to guarantee the continuation in office of the magistrates recently proposed by Baylón, and the other stipulated that the portion of federal funds to the states which the states must pass on to the municipal level (*participaciones*) be increased from 20 to 35 percent. Both measures were designed to force Ruffo into agreements which he might not wish or be able to keep. In the matter of raised municipal financing, which, as we will observe later, Ruffo advocated in principle, the main protagonist was a state legislator who had just recently been elected municipal president of Mexicali—none other than Milton Castellanos Gout.

Given that this was the PAN's first opportunity to formulate an economic development plan for implementation at the state level, it is worthwhile to determine the extent to which this plan (the Plan Estatal de Desarrollo, 1990–1995) differs significantly from those of PRI governments. Does it reflect a fundamentally different philosophy to that of the PRI? And how far does it correspond with the PAN's own traditional orthodoxy, given that this also is changing? In some respects the PAN's development plan is disappointing since, like most development plans in Mexico, it fails to set forth a new approach to controlling and directing social and economic development (Guillén López 1993: 94). Nevertheless, it does differ from its predecessors in several important respects. Unlike most PRI documents, which generally allude to the revolutionary goal of social justice, the PAN plan eschews social and class-inspired ideological themes. The PAN project aims to roll back state intervention, such that the state's role is limited to one of support and promotion, not implementation. Sectoral organizations are set aside, and the social base is envisioned as a more uniform citizenry which the state seeks to support through civic organizations or at the level of the individual.

The Baja California government program for 1989–1995 espoused major changes in the political system (see Baja California 1989). In its campaign platform, the PAN advocated modifying the state's political, economic, social, justice, and environmental systems which, the party argued, hampered the state's advancement and modernization. Specifically, the platform called for more decentralization (a topic to be discussed below); an improved relationship between the state and federal governments; upgraded water and housing services; better education for all Baja Californians; increased economic development; better environmental policies; and modifications to the justice system. Once elected, of course, Ruffo was obliged to narrow his focus somewhat. According to Oscar Padilla Fitch, former state director of public relations, Ruffo and his political loyalists have concentrated most of their energy in four areas: (1) housing and access to land; (2) the justice system; (3) water and sewerage provision; and (4) education. These areas, he said, were those most in need of attention. In the following sections we assess Ruffo's achievements in these four areas. Our purpose is not so much to measure his successes and failures, but rather to illustrate that a different philosophy of governance has shaped how Ruffo's administration has prioritized and sought to execute public policy—in short, that there has been a sea change in how Baja California has come to be governed under the PANistas.

Housing and Infrastructure

Governor Ruffo has attempted to improve living conditions in the state by initiating new housing development projects. In his second State of the State address on October 1, 1991, Ruffo announced that the demand for land for housing was expected to be met by the first semester of 1992. Ruffo noted that the distribution of land titles had increased from 9,152 in 1990 to an estimated 10,333 in 1991. Almost 300 housing projects had been completed in the state's four municipalities.[10] Furthermore, the government had encouraged the private sector to play a key role in providing housing, and this sector had responded by agreeing to build almost 2,000 housing units for the upper strata of the working class (950 units were completed in 1991).

Potable drinking water and improved sewerage continue to be among Ruffo's highest priorities, particularly in Tijuana and Mexicali. The program encompassing these two services is the most ambitious program in terms of public investment, receiving 266.7 billion old pesos[11] (U.S.$83 million[12]) in 1991, approximately 67.2 percent of all state resources received through a federal-state development agreement (a *convenio único de desarrollo*, CUD).[13] In an attempt to increase services, the state has begun constructing aqueducts in various towns—projects which represent a further investment of 109 billion old pesos (U.S.$36.5 million). Ruffo has also made an effort to improve water distribution networks, investing U.S.$23 million in Tijuana; U.S.$1.5 million in Ensenada in fourteen public works projects; U.S.$9.2 million in thirteen public works projects in fifteen neighborhoods; and U.S.$260,000 in five neighborhoods. Sewerage networks have also been extended in Mexicali and Ensenada. An investment of U.S.$3.1 million has helped support twenty-one public works projects in Ensenada.

---

[10] "Projects" often refer to "actions" which may be somewhat more limited in scope—such as the maintenance or improvement of existing housing development and so on.

[11] "Old" pesos became "new" pesos on January 1, 1993, when three zeros were taken off; i.e., 1,000 old pesos became one new peso. For standardization and for comparability purposes, we have usually indicated the U.S. dollar equivalent.

[12] All conversions to U.S. dollar equivalents are approximate and predate the peso devaluations that began in late December 1994, following the Mexican government's decision to allow the peso to float freely in international currency markets.

[13] For almost twenty years CUDs have represented the formal agreements between federal and state governments around which resources are transferred for agreed-upon projects. In principle, each governor includes in his plan the various local projects proposed by municipal presidents. These agreements have provided the basic framework for a variety of programs targeted to promote regional development, including major urban planning projects. Under President Salinas the CUDs were renamed social development agreements (*convenios de desarrollo social*).

Education and Justice

One of Ruffo's main priorities following the 1989 election was education. In 1990–1991, as reported in Ruffo's second State of the State address, there were approximately 14,300 students in preschool, 94,700 in elementary school, and about 37,800 in high school. With the number of students increasing and the conditions of the schools deteriorating, and with the federal government about to undertake a major program of decentralization of public education to the states, Ruffo's team of administrative and education experts attempted to make the modifications required to provide a better education system in Baja California. The new state secretary for education, Rafael Ayala López, initiated reforms to improve the schools. In 1989, at the beginning of Ayala López's tenure, 46 percent of the total state budget went to education, and almost all of these funds (97 percent) were spent on salaries and fringe benefits. Maintenance, school supplies, and repairs were virtually ignored. As a first step toward reducing the level of recurrent costs, Ayala López initiated a hiring freeze.[14]

A major conflict ensued with the National Union of Education Workers (SNTE).[15] Although the SNTE was very influential locally, it had suffered a major blow when its PRI lobbyist was defeated by Dolores de Méndez (of the PAN) in the elections to the state congress. The SNTE was also weakened when Ruffo cut back on personnel who were working for the union but were being paid out of state funds and when he closed and consolidated some schools. Moreover, Ruffo ordered elementary schoolteachers who lacked valid diplomas to attend night school before they could be considered for promotion. Ruffo's initiatives created a major arena for political conflict, but they seem to have been driven by pragmatic, not partisan, considerations. Ruffo recognized that he could ill afford to expend such a large slice of state resources on a single sector, and certainly not for recurrent costs. If he were to have any room for maneuver, he needed to break the SNTE's stranglehold on the budget.

Today, 48 percent of the state budget continues to be allocated to education. Baja California is the state with the highest expenditure per

---

[14]The education budget continues to put a large hole in the state's overall budget and in the shared revenues transferred from the federal government. In 1992, after the education decentralization reform was implemented, basic education in Baja California absorbed 67 percent of the funds the state received from the federal government. Compare this figure to the much lower proportion spent on education in poorer states: 52 percent in Veracruz, 25 percent in Michoacán, 19 percent in Puebla, etc. (*Revista INDETEC* 83 [July–August 1993]: 98).

[15]The SNTE is one of the most important and powerful national labor organizations covering teachers and staff in the education sector (see Cook 1990; Fowleraker 1993). Since President Salinas forced the removal of its authoritarian general secretary, Carlos Jonguitud Barrios, in 1989, the union has revitalized itself under the leadership of Elba Ester Gordillo, a leading PRIísta. For the 1994 elections, the SNTE's cross-party political action committee organized a national campaign to monitor the electoral process.

capita in this sector. Despite decentralization of the education system in 1992, teachers' wages continue to be negotiated in Mexico City, even though the states also bear some of the costs associated with salary increases.[16] Although the federal government has increased its funding to the state, Baja California remains responsible for 50 percent of higher education costs and 40 percent of elementary school costs. According to Eugenio Elorduy Walther, the state secretary of finance, the state's contribution is unfairly high; in the rest of the country, 75 percent of these expenditures are covered by the federal government. Although transfers from the federal to the state level increased by 53 percent between 1990 and 1992, inflation rose by 75 percent and teacher salaries increased by 135 percent (interview with Elorduy Walther, March 12, 1993).

Information was scarce on Ruffo's initiatives in reference to the justice system. However, our findings suggest that Ruffo has undertaken some reform of the justice system by eliminating corruption and improving efficiency. As reported in Ruffo's second State of the State address, the judicial police is seeking to professionalize its services and to improve communications with the municipalities. Furthermore, almost U.S.$400 million has been invested in upgrading prisons and police equipment in Baja California's four municipalities.

State Government Performance: An Overview

There has been an important change in the approach to state-level governance in Baja California. The Ruffo administration prioritizes programs differently than did its predecessors, and its methods of implementation are also substantially different—more open, more efficient, and more careful to match budgets and actions. This economy notwithstanding, the state government has had to undertake deficit financing in order to cover its basic programmatic costs. This is the principal reason why education features so large on the agenda: the economies achieved in that sector determine the feasibility of developing programs in other arenas. Though many may fault the pace of Ruffo's reforms, it is undeniable that the state agenda has changed and continues to do so. Furthermore, concurrent with Ruffo's changes at the state level, local municipal presidents were also initiating reforms of their own. Not only did they enjoy more autonomy to pursue various projects; they also had the support of Governor Ruffo, a former municipal president who understood their concerns.

However, this autonomy was double-edged. City hall administrations were obliged to take on an increasing share of responsibility for service provision as these functions were decentralized; they were also given control to issue a wide range of licenses and to collect property

---

[16] There are approximately 14,000 teachers currently being paid out of state funds.

taxes (*Zeta*, December 24–30, 1992, p. 40A). But although there are now greater opportunities for municipalities to raise their own level of funding, this deflects responsibility from the state government.

Municipal-Level Policy Agendas and Performance

As discussed above, the municipalities of Baja California have been delegated more responsibility and authority under Ruffo. The legal and financial aspects of this decentralization process are discussed in detail in chapter 5; here we propose to describe some of the concrete results of municipal autonomy and changing patterns of city hall administration. Although the political dynamics and demographic conditions of each municipality have evolved in different ways, there are certain broad trends that may be observed across the three municipalities we studied. Whether these trends can be attributed to a particular party's policies, or are a reflection of the development of more rational responses to recent political and economic conditions in the area, is difficult to determine. Specifically, there is greater emphasis upon efficiency and accountability, decreased emphasis on paternalistic government, and a growing focus on an increasingly responsible citizenry.

In the past under the PRI, Baja California displayed many of the characteristics of state-community relations that have linked partisan politics and service delivery in other parts of Mexico (see Cornelius 1975; Hiernaux 1986; Herzog 1990). The political support from low-income communities has changed over time, shifting from lightweight and ad hoc partisan support, through patron-clientelism, to more routinized patterns of government intervention since the late 1970s/early 1980s (Ward 1986, 1993). Some argue that nationally, with the advent of PRONASOL, the Salinas administration instituted a new program of clientelism articulated through Solidarity committees (Dresser 1991). In Baja California, state-community relations had been strongly articulated through the corporatist sectors of the PRI, particularly through the former National Confederation of Popular Organizations (CNOP). Since the ascendancy of the PAN to the state government, however, the strength and articulation of these networks have been greatly undermined (Guillén López 1993). Throughout the 1980s, Mexico experienced a gradual advance toward democracy and citizen participation, and although these changes cannot yet be considered consolidated, the PAN in Baja California seems to be changing the profile of Mexican politics by not observing the traditional "parastatal" relationship with the office of the president. This rupture in the corporatist structure appears to be leading to the inevitable disintegration of the traditional networks of political partisanship, as well as fragmenting former vertical and clientelistic structures, thereby redefining relationships between government and society in Baja California (Guillén López 1992: 180–81). Instead, the PAN has sought to make the processes of decision making and resource allocation more transparent and more routinized. Ruffo has espoused a more logical and orderly system of resource allocation and service provision in order to reduce the discretionary and clientelistic distribution of goods of yesteryear and in order to reduce corruption, enabling more to be done for less (*La Nación*, February 3, 1991).

Although partisanship is not entirely absent, most officials we interviewed made a point that they "work for the city, not for the party"; and the focus upon administrative competence, rather than upon party loyalty, appears to translate into more reliable and efficient service provision in the municipalities. In Ensenada, in particular, where the PRI lost its hold on city government over ten years ago, the PRI's organized links to the grassroots have largely been broken. PAN municipal administrations appear to center more upon two types of relationships with civic society. First, they want to ensure that citizens are properly informed and follow established, routinized procedures, rather than expecting to engage in clientelistic pressure politics. Second, PAN administrations promote a relationship articulated with individual citizens, rather than through leaders or through corporatist affiliated organizations, and they encourage the formation of links through a new civic network starting with the subdelegate in the neighborhood. This person relays information to an area delegate who ultimately makes a request for assistance at the municipal level. This extension of municipal control into individual neighborhoods might easily be construed as an attempt to build up a partisan network; however, an effort is made to promote the delegates as municipal employees, not as party representatives.

The municipalities' 1990–1992 development plans basically include the same general objectives, such as creating more housing, improving social welfare and health, raising the quality of education and the educational infrastructure, cleaning up the streets, and reducing crime. However, the success of these programs depends largely on whether the municipalities achieve greater economic efficiency in delivering services. In Ensenada, for example, efficiency in service delivery has been evaluated on the basis of the minimization of economic costs and the maximization of economic benefits. Ensenada, also, is working on developing its port facilities so that the city can play a larger role in the local economy. Another key concern of PANista governments is one of image. Various attempts have been made to clean up the streets, both through regular garbage collection and through the relocation of street vendors to certain clearly defined venues. While many of Ensenada's main streets are noticeably cleaner today, thirteen neighborhoods (both PAN and PRI) in that city protested in August 1991 at all three government levels against the lack of government assistance; residents had been waiting more than a year for garbage collection and the removal of large amounts of sewage. By and large, however, Ensenada's ability to deliver services has been good, especially in the area of sewerage (see table 1.3).

Mexicali's municipal plan focuses on integrated rural development and municipal revitalization. The strategy for social development focuses on improving the quality of services and fulfilling urban development objectives. The focus on delivering services more effectively was underscored by the current municipal president's campaign slogan: "He can deliver" ("Sí sabe cumplir"). The PRI, too, in Mexicali at least, also appears to believe in good governance; as we discussed earlier, municipal president Castellanos Gout has come to be known for the efficiency of his administration. It has been suggested that the changes in the PRI are responses to the new political landscape. Servicing deficits are lower in Mexicali than in the other municipalities, and the level of services provision has generally improved since 1970 (table 1.3).

Tijuana's primary preoccupation has been to clean up the city, reducing the "wrong kind of tourism" and enforcing the law. For example, Tijuana has set a minimum age for patrons of bars, including the tourist favorites on Revolución Street. The purpose is to reduce the number of underage tourists who cross the border from California, mostly on weekends, to drink and stir up trouble. Many taxi drivers are opposed to the new regulations because they impact negatively upon their business, but PAN officials respond that part of their plan is to educate people about the right kinds of tourism and commerce for a cleaner and more efficiently run city.

Tijuana has also shown some success in lowering its servicing deficits, which is particularly laudable given the sharp population growth experienced in recent years (table 1.1). Nevertheless, while the absolute number of people receiving water, for example, has increased, no conclusive evidence was gathered which indicated the quality of water service being received. Despite the increased water provision, water quality remains substandard. Most tap water is not drinkable unless purified, and thus most people continue to buy large bottles of drinking water for home use. Although providing electricity is a less complicated and less expensive process than constructing water lines, many neighborhoods in all four municipalities remain without electricity up to this date. While electricity is usually the easiest of public services to obtain (through official or unofficial channels), several people with whom we spoke in Tijuana said that their neighborhoods were still without electricity after twenty years. They added that the PAN appears to be working on their behalf to gain access to more services.

Less Paternalism, More Citizen Responsibility

Ruffo's 1990–1995 development plan establishes his objective to promote "the people's control over their own future, and [the aim] is to establish the following preconditions which will facilitate popular participation: confidence in the legal system, as well as opportunities for oversight of public expenditure." Ruffo's aim is to convince the residents of Baja California that accountability for progress lies in the hands of both the people and the government.

In general, both the state and the municipal authorities encourage citizens to take an active role in guiding Baja California's social, political, and economic development. Statewide, municipal services are being provided in a more systematic manner than in the past, as demonstrated by the improved conditions of the individual municipalities. A theme of partnership, rather than paternalism, appears to prevail among the PANista administrations we studied. For example, in Ensenada the new administration has included among its goals to educate the people about local and urban politics so that they can better use the system to address their needs. The use of community partnership practices relieves the government of some responsibility. While the PAN claims that it is acting as a government, rather than as a party, when it encourages such community and individual participation, from our perspective the emphasis upon educating the public also carries paternalistic overtones. One of Tijuana's PANista federal deputies explained that the party's ultimate goal is for the citizens to be *empowered*: by being more informed, people will be capable of making their own decisions.

It appears that while the PRI in Mexicali has also modernized along similar lines, it has maintained many of its party-dominated corporatist structures and traditional political programs. Through its new Urban Popular Territorial Movement, the PRI appears to be trying to secure its bases of support. This program revitalizes grassroots organizations, encouraging them to elect their own leaders, choose their agenda items, and solicit community support via established channels. While community involvement is a component of this strategy, such involvement is generated and coordinated by PRI party leaders—a point to which we will return below.

Partisanship and Getting the Message Out

One important question that we have consistently raised in our research regards the degree to which policy formulation and implementation meet partisan political ends, whether or not that was the intent (Rodríguez and Ward 1992; Ward 1993, 1995). Policies may be guided by either a technical or a partisan rationale. To the extent that parties in power are successful in implementing a technical agenda and demonstrating "good government," they are likely to benefit at the polls. But we do not interpret the motivation behind this policy as being specifically partisan. Following Diesing (1962), we suggest that partisan political rationale is not based upon the particular merits of a proposal, but upon who proposes or opposes it. Actions that are likely to create political difficulties will be avoided, no matter how technically sound they may be. And policies and actions that will significantly advance party or individual interests will be promoted, notwithstanding their technical weakness or flaws. Ward has described the growing technical rationale adopted by the Mexican state in recent years, particularly in those sectors related to improving economic productivity (Gilbert and Ward 1985; Ward 1986).

The evidence derived from our analysis of PANista municipal governments in Chihuahua suggests that the PAN is less directed by partisan motives than is the PRI, but that the PAN is not blind to the partisan advantages of certain policy lines (Rodríguez and Ward 1992: chap. 5). The Baja California evidence tends to confirm this pattern. However, the fact that here we are dealing with a *state* government—where the stakes are higher, the governmental time frame longer, and the policy scope and responsibilities broader—raises the likelihood that partisan (or nontechnical) criteria may enter the equation. Traditionally, municipal urban responsibilities have been tightly defined and constrained, while states have far greater room for maneuver, particularly if they are not beholden to the president. As we have observed in this and the previous chapter, Ruffo and his staff believe that the best chance for PAN continuance in power lies in good governance, efficiency, and positive outcomes for the population of Baja California. For rather complex reasons, they eschew seeking to develop the party base as the best strategy.[17] Thus, for the most part, they have also steered clear of partisanship, but there are several areas (which we describe below) in which the party-political rationale does appear to have been a consideration.

One example was the attack on PRI-linked labor organizations of street vendors and taxi drivers in Ensenada and Tijuana (*El Mexicano*, August 22, 1989; January 19, February 15, April 25, 1990). By cutting through the representational organizations or individuals that formally acted as brokers in the distribution and approval of operating licenses, the local governments in effect undermined the PRI's ability to co-opt and control union groups. Today the link is individualized: worker–municipal official. No longer are licenses issued according to union membership, implicit party affiliation, or graft. Instead, more stringent

---

[17]Perhaps the principal reason is the lack of confidence that many Baja California party militants have in Ruffo's cadre. Some of these militants are tied to Rosas Magallón. Also, any attempt to bring the two sides together would first have to address the philosophical differences between them. At present these differences appear to be irreconcilable, both in Baja California and at the national level (Guillén López 1993: 142 ff).

criteria relating to competence and past experience are invoked, and greater controls are exercised over where an individual may undertake his or her trade. Of course, there are good technical justifications for this more "responsible" exercise of power, which may well have been paramount. But one must also recognize the strong partisan outcomes derived from the application of the new policy. Similarly, when the state government sought to reassert control over the education budget, the Ruffo administration dealt firmly with the PRI-affiliated SNTE. Here, too, positions taken by both sides in the conflict appear to have been motivated, at least in part, by partisan considerations.

Ruffo's dealings with the press appear to have been quite clearly partisan, even vindictive. As we observed in chapter 2, Ruffo received a good deal of negative coverage in the PRI-friendly press. Once in office, he could make reprisal. Ostensibly to quell corruption, Ruffo issued a list of journalists known to have been on the PRI's or the state government's payroll. Thus began an extremely rancorous period between governor and press, which many saw as Ruffo's first major mistake. Instead of quietly changing the rules of the game, Ruffo simply gave the press an excuse to go on the offensive, eventually bringing the entire press corps down on his back.

Nationally, the principal news media have been strongly supportive of the PRI and PRI governments and highly critical or partisan in their coverage of non-PRI politicians or public officials (Crespo 1995). In recent years there has been some liberalization, especially of the print media, but most of the principal newspaper chains remain heavily dependent upon the federal government for their survival (Riva Palacio 1993). This is not to deny the existence of several worthy newspapers and magazines which are genuinely independent. Luis H. Alvarez cited the presence of regionally important newspapers (such as *El Norte de Monterrey* and *El Diario de Yucatán*) as a critical factor in the PAN's relative strength in certain regions (interview with Alvarez, June 1992), providing an independent forum for debate and for an objective assessment of government actions—a key ingredient in the democratization process. Unfortunately, in Baja California such a forum is generally lacking, with two important exceptions: the weekly newspaper *Zeta* and, more recently, the local radio.[18]

Zeta's reputation as a critical voice is well known and will not be elaborated here. Less widely recognized, however, is the importance that local radio has assumed in promoting open discussion among the population, the government, and political candidates. Radio's influence rose in earnest in 1988 when PAN presidential candidate Manuel Clouthier bought airtime in order to broadcast his message. After the

---

[18] The press remains highly biased in its reporting. Papers such as *El Mexicano* no longer ignore Governor Ruffo, but they tend to focus primarily on the negative aspects of his administration.

1988 campaign, the trend toward using radio as a means to reach the grassroots quickened. Live call-in shows now allow citizens to speak out with anonymity and without fear of censorship, thus enabling the public to challenge the accuracy of press reports and official pronouncements. These radio programs have become an important forum for public debate over the activities and achievements of PANista officials in Baja California and elsewhere (*Wall Street Journal*, December 3, 1993, p. A15). During the 1988 campaign, candidate Ruffo frequently participated in these programs.[19] Radio stations are now in heated competition to include government officials in their call-in discussions. The PAN in Baja California, Chihuahua, and Sonora has embraced this "open-microphone" approach to maximizing airwave impact (interview with Francisco Becerril, state head of the PAN, January 13, 1993).

Furthermore, experience in radio can be an asset for a political figure, as demonstrated by the fact that two of the three PANista federal deputies were formerly radio announcers. Jorge Esparza Carlos, now congressional deputy for Baja California's 6th district, began his career as a talk show host. His popularity led several parties (the PRD, PDM, PAN, and PARM) to invite him to run for Congress on their slate. Esparza, who had no prior party affiliation, opted to run as a PANista (interview with Esparza Carlos, January 12, 1993). Ernesto Enciso Clark, PAN deputy for the 5th district, was involved in radio from the early 1960s. Enciso claims to be a pioneer in speaking out against bad government and asserts that his radio program should enjoy the freedom of expression guaranteed by the Mexican constitution. Enciso was a longtime PAN sympathizer; he became a party member in August 1991 and ran for the deputyship in 1992 (interview with Enciso Clark, January 13, 1993). Several top officials in the Ruffo administration pointed out during our interviews that radio is "the most effective way of communicating with the people." Ruffo uses it frequently to give progress reports.

Solidaridad and Voluntad

Two programs, Solidarity at the federal level and Voluntad at the state level, illustrate the differing approaches and capabilities of the PRI and the PAN. Both programs have roughly similar aims—to direct government funding to less developed areas in an attempt to help impoverished citizens.

---

[19]Few people in Baja California have much confidence in the local and regional newspapers as sources of accurate information. The PAN's view is that journalists were bought off by former PRIísta governments. Former PRIísta governor Xicoténcatl Leyva gave land to the news daily *El Mexicano* under terms so favorable that it was, for all practical purposes, a gift. Also, the PRI is suspected of supporting a number of small papers by holding multiple subscriptions; these papers supposedly would fold without government support. Because many journalists are on the PRI payroll, critical reporting is extremely unlikely (interview with former PAN deputy Borbón Vílchez, January 11, 1993).

The National Solidarity Program (PRONASOL), a huge federal program initiated by President Salinas in the late 1980s, became the trademark of his administration. Its budget grew from U.S.$680 million in 1989 to $950 million in 1990, $1.7 billion in 1991, and an estimated $2.2 billion in 1992 (Ward 1993). Solidarity is oriented toward specific projects. When unfulfilled community needs are identified, local committees propose projects (sewers, day care centers, parks, etc.) and submit applications to PRONASOL. If the project is approved, PRONASOL provides funding, which sometimes (but not always) is matched by state and municipal monies or by contributions from the beneficiaries. Solidarity exists in every state of Mexico; it is well publicized and has had considerable success in increasing benefits for those in need (see Cornelius, Craig, and Fox 1994).

Solidarity is not, however, a completely altruistic effort on the part of the Mexican national government, insofar as it has served to recover the electoral ground that the PRI lost in many regions in 1988 (Molinar Horcasitas and Weldon 1994; Fox and Moguel 1995). The Solidarity logo carries the PRI's colors, which are identical to those of the Mexican flag, and subliminally at least, it conflates government with PRI and nationalist sentiment (Ward 1993; Rodríguez and Ward 1994a). A member of the PRI observed that the state government in Baja California disapproves of Solidarity because it benefits the PRI. Governor Ruffo also expressed some concern about the program's political content, primarily because it involves direct federal intervention and bypasses state and municipal governments (interview with Ruffo, March 12, 1993). Indeed, he somewhat disingenuously sought to deny its existence at one point, arguing that PRONASOL funds formed part of the ongoing regional development program of the *convenio único de desarrollo* (discussed earlier in this chapter): "I signed the CUD. If the federal government wants to call it Solidarity, that's something else. What is clear is that PRONASOL as such does not exist in Baja California" (*El Mexicano*, June 4, 1992, p. 8). Another PAN government official believes that Solidarity is run in a very partisan fashion; he noted that "essentially it is another, smarter way to buy votes" (interview with Guillermo Trejo, January 1993). And Elorduy Walther, the state's secretary of finance, referred to the Solidarity committees as "parallel governments" (interview with Elorduy Walther, March 12, 1993).

In a recent study of the organization and performance of Solidarity committees in Mexico's northern border region, Contreras and Bennett (1994) analyze the extent to which PRONASOL articulates a new set of relations between government and society. While Solidarity aims to present new approaches, these authors found that the local Solidarity committees in Tijuana and Mexicali were based largely upon preexisting organizations and leaders (this was true for 74 percent of committees in Tijuana and 82 percent in Mexicali). In particular, existing leaders tended to carry over (66 percent in Tijuana and 63 percent in Mexicali) as leaders of Solidarity committees. In Mexicali, leaders tended to belong to unions or political parties before and after they joined Solidarity committees, while in Tijuana many leaders came from neighborhood organizations. The percentage of committee leaders with bases in neighborhood organizations was 12 percent for Mexicali and 31 percent for Tijuana. Finally, Contreras and Bennett observed that:

> The PRI's greater influence on the committees in Mexicali (a municipality governed by the PRI) is a factor in their more traditional structure and more centralized leadership style. In contrast, committees in Tijuana (a municipality ruled by the PAN and one in which Solidarity faces strong competition from local community support programs) reflect greater diversity in their organizational structure and greater decentralization in decision making since the presence of civil society and of noncorporatist organizations is greater (1994: 300).

Thus, although Solidarity may have a partisan element to it, it is grafted onto existing structures, not all of which are PRIísta or corporatist. To the extent that the latter structures have been weakened in places like Tijuana and Tecate, there is no evidence to suggest that PRONASOL has been run through the ailing organizations in order to revitalize them. Whether or not the nonpartisan civic structures that are used will stay nonpartisan remains to be seen.[20]

Bypassed by the National Solidarity Program, the state of Baja California responded by creating Voluntad, an organization designed to coordinate the social welfare efforts of different ministries, to educate, and to facilitate community development efforts (interviews with Guillermo Trejo, January 12, 1993, and Ernesto Ruffo, March 12, 1993). Voluntad formed its first interagency group in February 1991 and selected a neighborhood (coincidentally named Solidaridad) as its pilot project. The Ruffo government ostensibly chose this neighborhood because it was the first one to be regularized after the creation of Voluntad.

Unlike Solidarity, Voluntad seems to have very little recognition in Baja California. Contreras and Bennett (1994) found, for example, that 93 percent of their sample (which included Nuevo León) was aware of the PRONASOL program, although only 25 percent knew that a Solidarity project existed in their neighborhood. Though we

---

[20]Guillén López (1993), in an extended footnote to his monograph, describes the ineffectiveness of PRONASOL's Tierra de Solidaridad program in Tecate, at least as a partisan strategy to bolster the PRI in that city. As we observed in chapter 2, the PRI lost Tecate in the 1992 municipal elections. See also Molinar Horcasitas and Weldon 1994.

lack statistical data, we are certain that Voluntad does not have anything near that degree of popular recognition. Guillermo Trejo, former director of Voluntad, contrasted this program's lack of publicity with the large sums that Solidarity spends on promoting its projects. According to Trejo, Voluntad prefers to direct its resources to projects that benefit the community instead of toward publicity. The PAN has developed the slogan "You can do it" ("tú puedes") as a guiding principle for Voluntad and, as Trejo emphasized, the program encourages beneficiaries to get involved and take an interest in their community. Getting the job done is important, but the impact will last longer if it actively involves the local community.

One of the aims of Voluntad was to coordinate the various state ministries' efforts to provide services, given that the social services sector was fragmented, with each ministry fighting for a piece of the budgetary pie. With a coordinated program and a sectoral plan focused through Voluntad, the administration hoped that the social services sector would be more competitive and more effective. According to Trejo, Voluntad's 1992 budget amounted to U.S.$8 million. This came from the budgets of individual ministries (U.S.$3–4 million), the governor's special projects fund (U.S.$2 million), and contributions from the beneficiaries (U.S.$2 million). Trejo was unclear whether this is an assigned budget or whether it represents funding limits which may be accessed by Voluntad. We suspect the latter; although U.S.$8 million is a significant amount (though it pales by comparison to Solidarity's funding), we found little in the way of specific accomplishments beyond the pilot project described earlier. When we broached this subject with Governor Ruffo, he cited an extremely lightweight example of the sort of work undertaken by Voluntad—the formation of a local group for guitar lessons (interview with Ruffo, March 12, 1993). Moreover, a 1992 article in *La Nación* which described the Ruffo government's accomplishments in 1992 mentions Voluntad but gives no concrete accomplishment. We found this rather curious for a party whose leaders can often relate to the inch the amount of pavement laid during their administrations. Our impression is that Voluntad is pretty much a letterhead designed to counter PRONASOL.

A picture emerges of two programs with similar goals but very different approaches, images, and results. Solidarity clearly is better known. But if its (unstated) aim is to garner support (and ultimately votes), then the public's rather low level of association between Solidarity and local projects, as reported by Contreras and Bennett, should be of concern to PRONASOL officials. Voluntad appears to have succeeded in establishing an identifiably PANista approach, but this program has yet to demonstrate that it can produce any real accomplishments. Governor Ruffo recently appointed Jesús del Palacio Lafontaine to head Voluntad. Del Palacio Lafontaine is an accomplished administrator; under his tutelage, Voluntad may perform more effectively in the future.

Conclusion: Democratization through Good Governance?

As we have seen in the final sections of this chapter, the PAN is not totally adverse to adopting partisan strategies. On the whole, however, as the preceding discussion demonstrates, Baja California has become a more tightly run ship since the PAN displaced the PRI in 1989. Officeholders are being selected for their competence rather than their party loyalty; urban services are being provided in a more routinized fashion; policy making and implementation are more transparent and honest; the influence of partisan corporatist organizations has been eroded; and technically inspired changes and urban policy agendas are edging out those with a more partisan rationale.

Measured against these sorts of performance criteria, the PAN has demonstrated important differences with its PRI predecessors. The state and municipal governments have had to do more with less—due both to the problems created by the outgoing administration and to the severe fiscal constraints imposed by the elevated education budget and Ministry of Finance officials' unwillingness to modify their structure of allocations to the state. Moreover, the Ruffo government is staking the PAN's political future upon demonstrating good governance, rather than seeking to secure the party bases through partisan organization and development. Thus far this strategy appears to be working reasonably successfully: the PAN won the senatorial election in 1991 and, on balance, did well in the 1991 and 1992 elections. Nevertheless, the 1994 federal election results will have given pause for thought: good government may not substitute for a united and well-organized party, particularly if the PRI opposition fields a strong candidate in the upcoming 1995 gubernatorial election.

Along with PAN successes have come some significant failures as well. The Ruffo government has not been able to bring party militants into the governmental process. Rather, he has surrounded himself with like-minded neoPANistas, and the internal strife between the two groups has intensified instead of attenuating. Nor has the state government been successful in its demands for an increase in its share of federal allocations, notwithstanding protracted negotiations with the Ministry of Finance (to be discussed in chapter 5), and Ruffo seems reluctant to take his case to the Supreme Court (Vicencio 1994). Despite the need to effect economies through reductions in government staff, this has not happened, largely because it would engender conflict with labor unions. The government has been obliged to increase its deficit, and unless it is able to win its battle with the Ministry of Finance, one cannot see how this deficit might be reduced. Somewhat disingenuously, Ruffo has spoken out against PRONASOL and, although he finally was obliged to intervene personally in the disaster relief program following intense rains and flooding in Tijuana in January 1993, he failed to take full advantage of the federal funds and support that were offered. Finally, like any government leader, Ruffo has made some serious mistakes, such as aggravating relations with an already hostile press.

When we conducted the fieldwork for this study—approximately halfway through Ruffo's administration—it was still too early to assess fully the extent to which greater democracy is being articulated through government programs. Certainly, new structures of state-society relations are being forged; these appear to be more individualized, and the role of often authoritarian local bosses and leaders has been reduced. There is greater efficiency and transparency in government, and services and resources are disbursed according to agency routines rather than following personalistic or partisan criteria. But in many respects the fact that these differences are notable reflects upon the poor governance exercised by state and municipal authorities prior to 1989. It is not so much a reflection of the PAN presenting an imaginative new approach—certainly not to be compared with the rather more sharply defined municipal governance we observed in Chihuahua (Rodríguez and Ward 1992).

Moreover, now that the PRI is operating more efficiently and openly in Mexicali, any differences that once existed are tending to fade. There may well be greater democracy in local government, but it is not the preserve of the PAN. Nor is it necessarily the case that well-run cities are better *governed* cities, although our assessment thus far suggests that there is greater public participation in urban affairs, along with greater financial transparency and accountability of public officials—all elements of better government, we believe. In the following two chapters we propose to intensify our analysis of democratization in Baja California, looking less at performance criteria of programs and actions (i.e., running the city and the state) and focusing more on whether there is "better government" (as measured by the institutional structures of government) and whether intergovernmental relations are changing in ways that are conducive to greater democracy.

4

Intragovernmental Relations: The Separation of Powers

Introduction: Powers and Real Powers

In this study of the incipient process of democratization unfolding in Baja California, chapter 2 focused on the electoral arena, arguing that increasing levels of political competition in the state facilitate the democratization process. Yet the emergence of democracy clearly requires much more than electoral competition. Institutions are also needed to represent and implement the people's will on a more regular basis than elections allow. In this chapter, we focus on the relationships among the separate branches of power at the state level and within city councils. We argue that at the state level, one can observe the exercise of a genuine separation of powers among the executive, legislative, and judicial branches. Similarly, at the municipal level, growing independence of city councils from their municipal presidents and increased debate within city governments are also indicative of an emerging separation of powers. Both processes are the outcome of improved opportunities to check the actions of the various powers (particularly those of the local executive). Our argument is that these developments are conducive to greater democracy in Baja California. But before turning to the particulars of the case study, we will briefly situate the notion of separation of powers within the larger body of democratic theory.

Democratic theory is concerned with the processes by which ordinary citizens exercise control over their leaders (Dahl 1956: 3). Usually this control operates through the popular election of representatives. However, if power becomes concentrated in the hands of the executive, the legislature, or the judiciary, then the external checks (usually elections) by which citizens hold their government accountable are reduced or altogether eliminated. One way to preserve accountability is through the separation of powers. If governmental power is fragmented, then each power will operate as a check on the others. In the United States, for example, the constitution of government at different levels—city, county, state, and federal—is predicated upon no level completely dominating another. As a further protection, classic democratic theorists such as Montesquieu and Locke held that officeholders in the different branches should be selected by different constituencies, through different procedures, and for different terms in office.

According to Nettie Lee Benson, Mexico's federalist system was informed by a need to unify increasingly autonomous provinces: "Contrary to the common belief that federalism was suddenly forced upon a unified country, impractically splitting it asunder, it was adopted in Mexico in 1823 because it was the only possible way to unite and solidify a country which, under the influence of a Spanish institution, had broken up into independent provinces that were verging on becoming independent states or nations" (1958: 90). Since 1810 one deputy from each of the (then) twenty-two provinces had participated in the Spanish Cortes. Each province was an independent political division responsible only to the Cortes, and the political chief in Mexico City had no control whatsoever over political chiefs elsewhere (Benson 1958: 92). A debate ensued (initially in the Spanish Cortes and later in the provinces themselves) which lasted for more than a decade, focusing during the early years on the powers that these new provincial governments should assume and later on the nature of any confederation between the provinces and on the role of the congress (Benson 1958; de Gortari Rabiela 1994).

The tension was between the two opposing political traditions: executive power versus legislative supremacy (J. Rodríguez 1994). The government in Mexico City, with its nationalist pretensions, supported a strong executive, while regional and local interests sought a political project which would give them control of their territory and minimize interference from the center. Their justification was that in such a large and geographically varied country, only local representatives could understand local problems (de Gortari Rabiela 1994: 212). This discourse is especially illustrative for current debates about the desirability of creating a new federalism in Mexico and restoring paramountcy of the regions, and the issues of separation of powers discussed in the remainder of this chapter.

Under the federalist system framed in the 1917 Mexican constitution, political power is concentrated at the center, particularly in the hands of the president (Carpizo 1978). In this highly centralized system, power is, in practice, surrendered to the center, particularly to the executive branch, even though in theory paramountcy is given to the "free municipality" and to the states. Some federalist systems have developed a structure of checks and balances to ensure that preeminence is accorded to the local level (i.e., to ensure *vertical* decentralization) and/or to regulate the *horizontal* separation of powers between the three branches of government (V. Rodríguez n.d.). The system of checks and balances in the United States meets both objectives, although administrations vary in the degree to which they emphasize local responsibilities and in the extent to which the separate powers work effectively with one another or, alternately, become gridlocked. However, Mexican federalism does not yet display these features—neither decentralization nor separation of powers—to any significant extent. Nevertheless, as this chapter and the following one seek to demonstrate, these features are beginning to emerge in Baja California.

Luis Javier Garrido argues that the Mexican president, in addition to his constitutional powers, also exercises "metaconstitutional" powers (some of which were discussed in chapter 1). These metaconstitutional powers are the unwritten norms of the Mexican political system (Garrido 1989: 422; see also González Oropeza 1983). The Mexican president can act as a constituent power with the authority to amend the constitution, serve as chief legislator, establish himself as the ultimate authority in electoral matters, assume jurisdiction in judicial matters, and remove governors, municipal presidents, and state and federal legislators (Garrido 1989: 424). This combination of constitutional and metaconstitutional powers makes the Mexican president one of the most powerful heads of state in the democratic world (Puertas Gómez 1993: 6). The high degree of centralization at the federal level dramatically reduces the potential for the separation of powers to act as a system of checks and balances.[1]

While it can be argued that in recent years the Mexican Congress has become more independent and more proactive in initiating legislation, the national political system continues to be dominated by the president. Although major interest groups have had some influence on public policy, the existence of an "official" party, whose members are guided by the executive, has meant that the role of the national congress in actively shaping the political process has been minimal. Indeed, in the early 1970s one author described the role of the legislature as "minor and basically ceremonial and technical" (Needler 1971: 43). Most analysts

---

[1] It is important to note that separation of powers and checks and balances are separate ideas, both theoretically and practically. However, the constitutions of both Mexico and the United States call for three separate branches of government (executive, legislative, and judicial) to share power. This is distinct from European parliamentary systems in which the executive and legislative branches are fused and where the three branches often perform differentiated functions (see Huntington 1968). We believe that a system of fused powers (i.e., functions) requires checks and balances to ensure against the tyranny of one branch. Moreover, Mexico and the United States are federalist systems, constitutionally based upon popular sovereignty. Political accountability is, therefore, more difficult and requires an active system of checks and balances. We realize that the idea of checks and balances is often viewed as a distinctly American innovation. However, the constitutional structures of Mexico and the United States are sufficiently similar to merit discussion of the need for checks and balances in the Mexican political context.

agree that this situation must change if the process of democratization is to advance in Mexico (Graham 1993: 187). While the executive branch may be the focus of attention during a period of regime transition, it is the strengthening of the legislative branch that is crucial to the institutionalization of democratic processes.

Although Mexico's state legislatures, just as the national Congress, have historically been weak, governors are likely to find it more difficult to control their legislatures under conditions of interparty competition or when a dominant local faction refuses to acknowledge the authority of a governor imposed by outside authorities.[2] Although it may be an overstatement to say that state congresses have automatically approved initiatives coming from the governors, state congresses have not been, in the main, active influences on executive power. This pattern repeats at the municipal level, where municipal presidents have largely dominated city councils. If state and municipal legislative bodies are dominated by their executives and interparty competition does not operate as a constraint, then the application of checks and balances to prevent the concentration of power is unlikely, if not impossible. We will return to a discussion of Baja California's state and local legislatures below.

As noted earlier, the president's metaconstitutional powers grant him influence in the judicial as well as the legislative branch. The Mexican president appoints Supreme Court justices with the advice and consent of the Senate. He also makes appointments to the "autonomous courts" that head up special jurisdictions in electoral, administrative, tax, and agrarian matters (Puertas Gómez 1993: 8). These federal-level courts take precedence over both state and local tribunals, regardless of any local constitutional or statutory provisions that may contradict national law. Although state tribunals are responsible for determining the constitutionality of legislation, the Mexican Supreme Court has ruled that no such controversies can be tried by local authorities.

Thus, although a system of checks and balances exists in theory in Mexico, in practice, any measures to guarantee a separation of powers are overridden by the power of the presidency. In Baja California, where the direct ties between the president and past PRI-controlled state and local governments have been broken, we find a nascent exercise of these separate powers. In this chapter we argue that in the area of *intra*governmental relations, changes under PANista administrations in Baja California, at both the state and municipal levels, are operating in ways which we regard as conducive to the emergence of more democratic systems of government. In the following sections we look first at intragovernmental relations at the state level—focusing on the executive, legislative, and judicial branches—and then at the level of the munici-

---

[2]This is one alternative; another, as we saw in chapter 2, is for the aggrieved group to withdraw local party support for the nominee, and maybe for the disaffected candidate to run as an independent—sometimes successfully, letting in the opposition.

pality, concentrating on the relations between municipal presidents and their city councils. On the state level, we argue, the checks and balances offered by genuine electoral competition are leading to a growing separation of powers as mandated by the constitution. On the municipal level we discuss how increased debate in city government and the city councils' increased independence from municipal presidents have also allowed an incipient system of checks and balances to operate.[3]

Relations between the Governor and the State Congress

Baja California's state legislature is unicameral and includes nineteen representatives: fifteen elected from state districts and four elected through proportional representation. As we also noted earlier, the legislature's composition changed significantly in 1989, when the PRI lost its majority. Because no party had a majority in the 1989–1992 congress, parties had to join forces in order to pass legislation. According to Borbón Vílchez, PAN majority leader in the 1989–1992 state congress, there were a large number of split votes during his tenure. And PRI and PAN deputies sometimes abstained from voting or voted against their party.[4]

When invited to compare the PRI-controlled 1986–1989 legislature with that of 1989–1992, Borbón Vílchez claimed that the former congress had depended on the executive to initiate legislation. On only one occasion, he said, did a legislator propose a bill of his own devising (interview with Borbón Vílchez, January 11, 1993). Not surprisingly, Martina Montenegro, PRI minority leader in the 1989–1992 congress, differed with Borbón Vílchez over the extent to which the legislative branch was independent of the executive during the latter legislature, asserting that it continued to rely heavily on the executive branch for technical assistance and legislative initiatives. However, both legislators attested to an increase in the number of bills proposed by state deputies. During the 1989–1992 congress, Montenegro noted, PRI deputies proposed twenty-seven initiatives on *maquiladora* pollution control, worker pensions, and legislation to protect women, of which approximately 50 percent were eventually passed.

---

[3]Clearly, a genuine system of checks and balances in city hall ought to include additional components not discussed here (e.g., oversight of functions among the branches). However, because the functioning of checks and balances on the municipal level in Baja California has not yet been institutionalized, we can only point to what we consider to be first steps: increased levels of debate and of independence between members of city councils and municipal presidents.

[4]A much publicized case of division within the congress and the PAN itself was that of Dolores de Méndez, a PAN deputy. On February 12, 1992, de Méndez renounced her membership in the party because of differences with Borbón Vílchez. According to the press, she objected to the PAN deputies' practice of going off alone to plot strategy.

The extent to which legislatures generate legislation—as opposed to merely acting on initiatives coming from the executive—is an important issue if an argument for greater separation of powers is to be sustained. Certainly, the tradition in Mexico is that the role of national and state congresses be reactive and compliant, rarely amending legislation in any dramatic way (Camp 1993: 138). Our conversations with Borbón Vílchez and Martina Montenegro suggest that, from 1989 onward, members of the Baja California state congress began to play a more proactive role. Guillén López (1993: 121) is more circumspect in his interpretation: he notes that the executive continued to initiate legislation, especially in the important areas of human rights, environmental protection, and tourism. He attributes this to the fact that Baja California's congress is poorly equipped in terms of support staff and infrastructure, and many of its members lack political experience. Given that the PANista faction did not enjoy an outright majority, it hardly seems surprising that important legislative initiatives emanated from the executive branch rather than from the floor of the house. Moreover, this should not negate the state congress's significant shift toward an increased propensity to propose legislation after 1989.

As noted in chapter 2, electoral reform was one of the most vigorously debated topics in the 1989–1992 state congress. Following up on his 1989 electoral campaign promise to send a new electoral law to the legislature, Ruffo presented a preliminary version of the bill to congress soon after taking office, recommending that the state electoral commission be made independent of the legislative branch.[5] The PRI delegation rejected the bill, and the PAN could not persuade other parties to support the initiative. For most of 1990 and 1991, state electoral law and procedures were vehemently disputed as Ruffo attempted to pass reforms and political parties maneuvered to protect their positions. In September 1991, the PRD and the PPS rejected another version of Ruffo's proposed electoral law, claiming that it threatened minority parties.

Finally, in February 1992 an amended electoral reform law was passed, which included several of Ruffo's original proposals: public debates among all candidates (enhancing media access for all parties); allocation of 50 percent of the funds available for political campaigns, to be distributed in equal amounts to all political parties and remaining monies to be distributed to parties in proportion to the number of votes each obtained during the preceding election; and the institution of a voter photo identification card. It would appear that Ruffo considered making further changes to the electoral law; during the

---

[5]Under the existing electoral law the new congress would itself "approve" the election results, essentially validating its own election.

congressional elections of August 1992, he remarked on some irregularities remaining in the electoral process and proposed to correct them via modification to the electoral commission (*El Mexicano*, August 14, 1992).

Another indication of the separation of powers between executive and legislative branches was the legislature's decision to discuss Ruffo's first State of the State address (delivered just weeks after he assumed the governorship). This broke with tradition, by which the governor usually read his address to congress and the event was concluded without discussion. The following year Ruffo responded by advising that he would present his address in writing only. Opposition legislators objected, claiming that Ruffo had unilaterally broken with tradition and violated legislative rights and privileges. Also during the second year, the congress asked Ruffo to appear to respond to questions concerning his address, which he subsequently did.

There were other firsts during the 1989–1992 congress. The legislature exerted its authority vis-à-vis the governor by refusing four of Ruffo's nineteen recommendations for the judiciary. Traditionally, congress adopted the executive's nominations without question. Additionally, the congress for the first time publicly discussed the funding of state government; during its first year, the new congress reviewed the accounts of the previous government. Although the PAN was accused of attempting to defame the preceding PRI administration, the accounts issue captured the public's attention. People began to attend congressional sessions, something not done previously. This confrontation was significant because it sparked ideological debate and an unprecedented questioning of the executive branch by the legislature. Indeed, according to PAN majority leader Borbón Vílchez, during the 1989–1992 congress "just about everything was questioned, except the existence of God."

Prior to the 1989–1992 congress, there were four legislators per office, with space allocated on a first come, first served basis, and latecomers were often relegated to stairwells or hallways. This changed in 1989; all legislators received private offices, each equipped with a desk, filing cabinet, and telephone. In 1989, there was only one computer for the entire congress; at the end of the term in 1992, there were seventy. A congressional office was established in each municipality, with a fax machine and a modern telephone system, giving deputies a means to communicate with their staffs in Mexicali while they visited constituents in their home districts.

During the 1989–1992 session, the congress created a system of commissions and hired extra staff to help gather information with which to challenge the executive. The staff of the State Comptroller's Office, which advises the state congress regarding government accounts and programs, received additional personnel and upgraded equipment. Several deputies commented that these changes improved the legislators' access to independent sources of information, allowing congress to maintain a higher degree of independence from the executive branch.

The 1989–1992 congress did not hesitate to act when it disagreed with an executive decision. In June 1992, rates for water, electricity, and public transit were increased to offset skyrocketing operating costs and a reduction in federal subsidies. A number of PAN deputies joined with PRI and PRD legislators in opposition to these highly unpopular measures (which had been proposed by the executive branch) and eventually forced a retraction of the plan to increase bus fares (*El Mexicano*, June 5, 1992).

We might ask whether this new legislative profile can be attributed to increased competition between parties or, rather, to the institutionalization of a new role for the legislative branch vis-à-vis the executive. Our view is that the (sometimes conflictive) interactions that characterized executive-legislature relations from 1989 to 1992 occurred not only between competing political parties but also *between branches*. As noted above, PAN deputies voted against the governor and their own party on several occasions. Competing parties also joined PAN deputies frequently against executive initiatives. Although independent action on the part of branches of government is not a new institutional construct or process, what is new in this case is its high degree of activation.

Although we have focused primarily on the legislative and executive branches, changes have also occurred within the judicial branch. According to Governor Ruffo, the judicial branch has become freer of the executive since 1989. By law, the state's justices elect their own president. Yet Ruffo claimed that Baja California's judges were so accustomed to the governor selecting their president that Ruffo's refusal to choose a president took them by surprise. For two years, Ruffo said, the justices were constantly consulting with him on the merits of prospective candidates. They finally made their selection in the third year (interview with Ruffo, March 12, 1993). Indeed, the judges are now beginning to exercise their independence to such a degree that they are politicking among themselves for the presidency.

Another instance of checks and balances operating at the state level was a law passed on January 31, 1993, creating the Office of the State Attorney General for Human Rights (PDH). The office's mandate is to ensure that all citizens of Baja California receive the full protection guaranteed by the Mexican constitution and the Universal Declaration of Human Rights. Its Human Rights Commission will review cases of alleged human rights abuses and recommend remedies. It will act as a check within the system, since it is solely responsible to the congress. Only the congress can remove members of the PDH; the executive may not.[6] According to the director of the PDH for Mexicali, Federico García Estrada, the PDH is, in effect, an agency of the congress.

To conclude, a genuine separation of powers is emerging in Baja California. This is not to say that it did not exist before 1989, although in practice this separation was rarely visible and never ongoing. Now it is both visible and persisting, providing a means by which checks and balances can be activated and articulated.

Municipal President–Municipal Council Relations

In this section we examine intragovernmental relations at the municipal level in Ensenada, Tijuana, and Mexicali. Strictly speaking, one cannot talk of a true separation of powers, since the city council is a collegiate body elected on the same slate as the municipal president (which today embraces some minority party participation). The council's functions are both legislative and "watchdog" (Ochoa Campos 1986), and both functions must be exercised if real democratization is to occur within city hall—the level at which government impinges most importantly upon people in their daily lives.[7] The operation of checks and balances may be measured by examining the amount of debate within the city council and the degree to which the municipal president and his appointed executive officers are made accountable to the elected members of the city council. Our view is that council members' increasing independence from municipal presidents and the heightened levels of debate are indicative of greater democracy in government. Under opposition governments in Ensenada (since 1983) and Tijuana (since 1989), city council members have assumed a more active role in challenging municipal presidents. And in Mexicali, where the PRI has consistently dominated, our interviews also uncovered an increasing degree of internal democratization on the city council.

Mexico's constitution and laws emphasize the "free municipality" (*municipio libre*) which in theory has autonomy over its own affairs. However, as mentioned earlier, Mexico's highly centralized political system has historically prevented municipalities from exercising this independence. The municipality is governed by a city council (*ayunta-*

---

[6] However, according to Guillén López (1993: 125), the executive proposes at least two names to congress from which congress members must select one.

[7] "The municipality is the training ground for democracy in Mexico because it is the political institution which has the closest contact with the people. Democracy is understood as the people's participation in the decisions which affect them; it is a system based on a continuing improvement in the population's economic, social, and cultural conditions" (from the text "El Municipio Mexicano" [Centro Nacional de Estudios Municipales, 1985], cited in *Estudios Municipales* 10 [July–August 1985]: 236).

miento) headed by a municipal president who serves a three-year term. In addition to the municipal president, the city council includes appointed officials and one or two trustees (*síndicos*) and several councilmen (*regidores*), whose number is set by the respective state constitution. When all elected members of the city council meet in full session, they constitute the *cabildo*, the highest decision-making body of a municipality, with authority to approve all plans, programs, projects, and budgets within the municipality.

Traditionally, PRI municipal presidents were handpicked by higher ups within the party/government apparatus (congressmen, the state governor, and local party chiefs). Not surprisingly, this has been a source of conflict within municipalities; municipal presidents chosen by the incumbent governor or by outside party leaders are often unpopular with the general public, local politicians, and the council itself because of their inept handling of local problems (Cornelius and Craig 1991: 26). However, local PRI leaders (especially the PRI's municipal secretary) generally expect to have the lead voice in selecting the council candidates who appear on the same slate as the municipal president.

Once elected, the municipal president has nearly total control over the appointment of his municipal officers—treasurer, secretary, public works chief, etc. These appointed officials constitute the executive wing of the town council; within the guidelines laid down by the municipal president (at whose convenience they serve), they enjoy considerable autonomy over their agendas and programs. Not surprisingly, would-be municipal presidents who have some independent political weight (and are, therefore, in a position to negotiate) insist on placing their own people on the slate[8] in order to avoid possible problems further down the line.[9] The council members monitor the municipal president and his appointed officers' activities and they periodically approve budgets, but usually the municipal president is able to negotiate his officers' programs through council meetings. In fact, one of the municipal president's principal tasks is to negotiate his policy agenda, particularly when the council members of the opposition close ranks and/or join forces with members of his own party to oppose him. We now turn to our three municipalities, where we will see that there have been important changes in this relationship.

---

[8] One example is Francisco Barrio in Ciudad Juárez in 1983 (Rodríguez and Ward 1992).

[9] In our view this is a serious flaw which undermines any separation of powers between executive and the collegiate body of the municipal council. It seems essential that if there is to be a separation of party and government at the level of the city government, then independence of the council should not be left to chance but should be legislated for, either by having council members elected *in their own right* (i.e., not as one of an "all or nothing" slate tied to the candidate for municipal president) or by choosing some council members to stand as representatives for different spatial entities within the municipality. This would resemble the district elections of city council members in the United States, some of whom are elected by district while others are "at large."

Ensenada: Dissension in the City Council

Ensenada provides a clear example of how council members assert their power vis-à-vis the municipal president, particularly in the 1989–1992 period.[10] In this triennium, the city council established itself as an outspoken and critical body. In fact, ex-municipal president Jesús del Palacio Lafontaine noted that everyone, including council members, had the right to express a point of view and that strict party discipline was not required. According to del Palacio, it was his responsibility to build a majority on key issues. He noted that he generally obtained the necessary votes for key components of his program and that sometimes even the PRI council members voted with him. Former councilman Jorge Antonio Catalán Sosa affirmed that there was genuine decentralization of power between 1989 and 1992, as council members attempted to increase their participation in the city government's decision-making process, to reduce the municipal president's paternalistic control over the governing process, and to increase citizen awareness of the role that council members could play in municipal government (interview with Catalán Sosa, January 13, 1993).

To some extent, the council members did succeed in asserting their independence from the municipal president. On January 16, 1991, in a particularly heated council meeting, trustee councilman Carlos Silva Tonche (PRI) was removed, allegedly for poor performance. Attending the meeting were Silva Tonche, municipal president Jesús del Palacio, and the ten councilmen. The meeting lasted six hours and ended in a 6-to-5 vote in favor of terminating Silva Tonche (*El Mexicano*, January 16, 1991). The opposition was led by Jorge Catalán and Mario Galaviz, both of the PAN, who, according to *El Mexicano*, accused Silva Tonche of fraud and incompetence. Less than six months later, *El Mexicano* reported that several council members and trustee Sidón Pérez also accused Silva Tonche of fraud in two vehicle auctions (*El Mexicano*, June 10, 1991). However, Santos Molina (current municipal president) claims that the

---

[10]From 1986 to 1989, our newspaper analysis uncovered few instances of conflict between the city council members and Ernesto Ruffo, municipal president at the time. In fact, according to the newspaper reports, there were only three instances of conflict between the executive and the council. On December 8, 1986, *El Mexicano* reported that some members had complained about Ruffo's appointment of Fernández Bandini as the councilman in charge of sports because of his supposed lack of sports knowledge and claimed that another candidate had more experience. On February 18, 1987, Councilman Rubén López Simental (PRI) accused Ruffo of violating the rules by being absent without the council's permission and by naming municipal delegates without following legal requirements (*El Mexicano*, December 31, 1987). Finally, on March 3, 1987, Rubén López Simental accused Ruffo of violating his rights as a councilman by trying to limit a meeting of the city council to members of the PAN. López Simental asserted that if the PAN council members wished to meet alone, they should not gather on government property. In fact, the extent of actual independence exercised by council members vis-à-vis the municipal president during this period is probably somewhat overstated. Certainly we found little evidence of disagreement or internal conflicts being reported in *El Mexicano*, which, given its anti-PAN stance, would almost certainly have alighted upon any occasion it could find.

real reason for Silva Tonche's removal was his failure to meet the residency requirements for the position of trustee. Because PANistas tend to follow rules to the letter, according to Santos Molina, Silva Tonche's shortcoming in this regard was sufficient cause to have him removed. Regardless of the actual reasons for Silva's dismissal, the important consideration is that he was removed over the objections of the municipal president and several PAN council members, illustrating that the city council had begun to exert its independence from the executive.[11]

While these increased degrees of independence between components of the city government are suggestive of longer-term changes in the methods of municipal governance in Baja California, the question of whether there has been an effective institutionalization of the separation of powers cannot be adequately addressed under the current electoral rules, or until an alternation in power has occurred. Nevertheless, the extended period over which these changes have taken place (eight years), the electorate's continued preference for the PAN's approach to governance, and the inclusion of nonparty loyalists in preeminent elected positions in municipal government (such as ex-municipal president Jesús del Palacio Lafontaine, who did not become a party member until well after assuming office) all seem to point toward the continuation of these changes in Ensenada, regardless of the PAN's future electoral success.

Tijuana: Conflict in the Council

An interesting twist in the development of checks and balances has emerged recently in Tijuana's municipal government. At first glance, Tijuana appears to have experienced growing debate within its city council during the 1989–1992 session rather similar to that in Ensenada. However, upon closer inspection the debate could more accurately be characterized as intraparty conflict rather than as an exercise of checks and balances between the city council members and the municipal president. Under municipal president Carlos Montejo Favela (PAN), council members enjoyed a great deal of independence. The battles that occurred were waged between "old" and "new" PANistas, with their distinct approaches to governance. Widely publicized by the media, these conflicts within the city council began immediately after Montejo Favela took office, and he described them as the most difficult problem he faced during his administration. The conflict in Tijuana during this period centered around two opposing camps: Montejo Favela and his

---

[11] It is interesting to note that PANista councilmen joined with the PRI council member in opposing the municipal president and other PANistas. In another incident it was the PANista councilmen who denounced del Palacio for purchasing municipal goods from his own business organizations or from others with whom he had close association (*Baja California*, October 23, 1990, p. 1).

supporters, and the so-called *magallones*,[12] followers of Salvador Rosas Magallón, a key actor in the history of the PAN in Baja California. For over four decades Rosas Magallón participated in marches and protests of every kind, especially against perceived electoral fraud. Although Baja California was the primary focus of his activities, Rosas Magallón gained national attention. On four occasions (1964, 1970, 1976, and 1987) his name surfaced as a precandidate for the PAN presidential nomination. In many ways Rosas Magallón worked to keep the opposition alive in Baja California, even at the price of spending time in jail in Mexico and in self-imposed exile in the United States. Knowing this history, one would expect Rosas Magallón to be pleased with Ruffo's win of the Baja California governorship in 1989. Yet during the first four years of PANista government at the state level and in Tijuana (where he resides), Rosas Magallón distanced himself from the PANistas in office. According to Rosas Magallón, the PANistas now in government have lost touch with the party's ideological and historical roots. He claims that these PAN functionaries (sometimes referred to as neoPANistas) are in office only for power and material gain.[13]

The *magallones* severely criticized Montejo Favela for wanting to raise property taxes, for making overly restrained cuts in the salaries of political functionaries, and for overspending and mismanaging municipal funds. Local, state, and even national newspapers eagerly reported on the internal bickering (*Proceso*, February 17 and June 8, 1992). In October 1990, *El Mexicano* reported an incident in which the *magallones* questioned an expenditure of 513 million pesos by the municipality without city council authorization (*El Mexicano*, October 15, 1990). On December 5, 1991, *El Mexicano* publicized the case of two PAN councilmen who claimed to have proof of financial impropriety within the municipality. And Rosas Magallón, now writing a column for the weekly

---

[12]Montejo Favela registered in the party ten minutes before officially announcing his candidacy for the municipal presidency, and he himself claims that the *magallones* invited him to be the party's candidate because he had no base of support within the party and could, therefore, be easily manipulated. Representing the *magallones* on Montejo Favela's council were Juan Manuel Salazar and María Belén Rosas Magallón, Rosas Magallón's son-in-law and daughter.

[13]Interview with Salvador Rosas Magallón, January 14, 1993. Magallón's wish was to keep the PAN moored to the conservative ideas that led to the party's formation, namely, respect for the Catholic Church and a turn toward neoliberal economics. However, at both the national and local levels many PANistas have adopted pragmatic strategies in developing their political project, which are often in accommodation with the federal government. Moreover, the latter's neoliberal project, as well as the official recognition of the Catholic Church, has meant that part of the traditional ideological property claimed by the PAN as its own has now been adopted by the PRI, leading to a dilemma as to whether the PAN should intensify its own traditional position or swim with the tides of changing national government directions. The latter view, of course, is the one adopted by the national PAN leadership and by the majority of those in executive government positions at the state and municipal levels. The traditionalists, the so-called *foristas*, tend to be most heavily represented in the legislative branches of government and in some cases have left the party altogether.

Zeta, publicly declared that "irregularities persist in the Tijuana city government" (*El Mexicano,* August 7, 1991).

While PRIístas pointed to these conflicts within the council as evidence of the PAN's inability to govern, others saw the situation differently. Enrique Pérez Santana, municipal director of economic and social development from 1989 to 1993, said that whatever negative impressions such conflicts generated were due to the fact that the public is not accustomed to such internal dissent. The PRI-dominated councils of the past did not tolerate it. Consequently, the public came to view any manifestation of conflict within a political party with some misgiving (interview with Pérez Santana, January 11, 1993). Similarly, Concepción López Serrano, a council member during Montejo Favela's municipal presidency, described the conflicts as a difference in methods of governance. The *magallones,* she said, "seized on the letter of the law. Montejo, in contrast, sought to compromise in order to arrive at an acceptable solution." She agreed that the public is not used to seeing this type of open political conflict. "We learned the hard way," she said; "most of us supporting Montejo in the city council were not experienced politicians, but came from all walks of life" (interview with López Serrano, January 12, 1993).

Regardless of the reasons behind the conflict, most observers would concur that it did hurt the PAN. Indeed, it is hard to see how this type of debate and discussion furthered democracy in Tijuana at all. Both Montejo Favela and the PANista council members expended much of their energy fighting internal battles. While the *magallones* and neo-PANistas both claimed to be authentic representatives of their party, neither governed as effectively as they might otherwise have done. Many observers believe that these conflicts contributed to the near defeat of the PAN in Tijuana in the 1992 elections. While the PAN just managed to hang on, the PRI made tremendous gains over their 1989 showing (see chapter 2).

The current PAN city council, headed by municipal president Héctor Osuna Jaime, has been carefully structured to avoid the division and conflict that occurred under Montejo Favela. Osuna admits that "Montejo committed many political errors," the most harmful of which was to allow his candidate slate to be taken over by people not loyal to him personally (interview with Osuna Jaime, March 14, 1993). Four of the nine PANista members of the current city council (1992–1995) have been active in the party for at least four years. Although Osuna did not insist on a particular slate of candidates, he did require that the council members, in addition to being loyal party members, be committed to avoiding the internal divisions and politicking that plagued the previous administration. When we questioned Osuna as to whether he favored pragmatists or ideologues on the city council, he responded "a mixture of both." When asked to comment on his relationship with the council members, Osuna insisted that he maintains an independent position: "They don't owe me anything, and I don't owe them anything," implying genuine independence for and from his council members. Future research will reveal if the intraparty conflict during Montejo Favela's administration was a step toward institutionalizing a system of checks and balances within the municipality or merely a temporary aberration in the process of democratization in Baja California.

Mexicali: Control of the City Council

We turn last to Mexicali, currently the sole PRIísta municipality in Baja California and, therefore, an interesting test case for evaluating the extent of democratization at the municipal level. Our impression is that municipal government in Mexicali under the PRI during the 1989–1992 period also demonstrated greater democratization within the city council, albeit perhaps with less tolerance for a plurality of views than in the two cases previously described. Although the municipal president continues to dominate municipal government, there is evidence of increased debate between the municipal president and council members. Forced to confront rising electoral competition, the PRI government in Mexicali has adopted new strategies in order to maintain power and come to rely increasingly upon technical administration. However, it is an open question as to whether the changes occurring in Mexicali can be partially attributed to former municipal president Milton Castellanos Gout's personal style, or whether they reflect other structural factors.

Castellanos Gout played a dominant role in many of the changes occurring in Mexicali from 1989 to 1992. His father was a former governor of Baja California, and he himself is well connected to prominent PRI officials throughout Mexico. However, it appears that government officials within his administration did not gain posts based upon loyalty alone; they also had to demonstrate significant administrative abilities. Efficiency emerges as an important theme of Castellanos's administration. During his tenure, the system of record keeping was modernized, allowing the municipality to collect seven times the previous tax base; the police department attempted to improve the standing and behavior of its force; and the municipality sought to accomplish more with a lower level of state funding. Although Castellanos introduced a greater level of technical and administrative efficiency into municipal government, he continued to keep a firm hand upon an increasingly assertive city council.

During the 1989–1992 period, Castellanos Gout set the municipal agenda in a straightforward, top-down manner, occasionally consulting with the city council on details of delivery and distribution, but with little discussion as to timetables and the ranking of priorities. Not surprisingly, he characterized intra-council relations as positive, claiming that the opposition voted with the PRI majority so often that more than half of the council votes were unanimous. Ex-councilman Armando Martínez Gámez (PRI) agreed that opposition members frequently fell in line with the majority, but he added that the opposition often differed with the majority. Both PRD and PAN council members mentioned that at times even PRIístas would cast opposition votes.

Not surprisingly, interviews with PRD council members concerning relations on the council also contradict the municipal president's upbeat description. PRD council members said that Castellanos Gout had inflated the number of unanimous votes. Abstentions, they asserted, were not counted when calculating unanimity. And opposition members often received key documents just thirty minutes before a vote was scheduled, leaving insufficient time to review the materials. Further, while opposition members were formally seated on various council committees, in at least one case (that of Sylvia Beltrán Goldsmith) the opposition member was never told when the committee was scheduled to meet, enabling PRI members to control the meetings. Although there were no cases in which the council rejected a Castellanos Gout initiative, there is evidence that council members (both PRIísta and opposition) did vote against the municipal president on occasion. And although they were not prepared to allow full-fledged disagreement, members expressed evidence of some limited debate within the council.[14]

Conclusion: Democratization through Intragovernmental Opening

At the state level in Baja California, our evidence reveals an increasing separation of powers among the three branches of government since 1989. Democratic theory suggests that active checks and balances built into a functioning system will enhance the separation of powers. In the past, the lack of competitive elections and the heavily centralized political system and presidential powers in Mexico have meant that the checks and balances built into the federal system have not been activated to any significant extent—at least not until recently. It is the induction of opposition parties into government that has broken the mold. It is an open question whether greater electoral competition and a more vibrant national congress alone will be sufficient in and of themselves to prompt a greater separation of powers in the center. The trend since 1988 has been toward this outcome, but at the same time there are clear indications that presidentialism has intensified rather than attenuated, as observers would expect if the country were undergoing genuine democ-

---

[14] Also because of rising electoral competition from the PAN in Mexicali, there appears to have been a tendency among the PRI to close ranks, leading to greater party loyalty than usual. This also helps explain the relatively limited debate within the city government.

ratization (Meyer 1993).[15] Nationally, it has probably been more a process of two steps forward, one step back.

However, in Baja California, the election of a PAN governor committed to horizontal—and vertical (see chapter 5)—decentralization as articulated through the separation of powers has led to the possibility of opening up the political system and activating the checks and balances latent within it. We view these developments as facilitating greater democratization in Baja California. On the municipal front, we have observed increased levels of debate between the municipal president and the city council and greater independence of one from the other. In Ensenada, it appears that the system has not only been strengthened but that the process of institutionalization has begun. Although incipient signs attest to the long-term sustainability of this process in Tijuana and Mexicali, more time is needed before any definitive conclusions can be reached. Equally important, at the state level the legislative and judicial branches exercised greater independence from the executive branch during the 1989–1992 period. Finally, there is greater participation and public involvement in all levels and branches of government in Baja California.

In the following chapter we extend this argument to the arena of *inter*governmental relations, that is, the municipalities' increasing autonomy from the state government. In large part this independence is a result of decentralization, which now allows municipalities to administer many programs and activities previously controlled by the state. The transfer of key governmental responsibilities from the state to the municipal level represents a significant change in intergovernmental relations in Baja California and in Mexico.

---

[15]The examples most often cited are: the continuation of the *dedazo* system of candidate selection; the removal of governors and the reversal of gubernatorial election outcomes; greater fiscal centralization; and Solidarity programs being run discretionally out of the president's office (until 1992).

5

Democratization through Decentralization: The Changing Nature of Intergovernmental Relations

In this penultimate chapter, we extend our discussion to relations between the federal, state, and municipal levels of government. Thus far we have argued a case for incipient democratization as measured through growing electoral competition and electoral reform, through new patterns of recruitment and less paternalistic and clientelistic relations with civic society, and through a growing separation of powers and a fuller functioning of responsibilities among various instances of government at state and municipal levels. The latter has begun to broach issues of autonomy and the decentralization of various functions of government to levels at which there is greater involvement in decision making by the wider populace, and greater transparency and accountability of elected and other government officials. In our view, decentralization, properly implemented, also goes to the heart of democratic principle.

The Theory: Dimensions of Decentralization

The scholarly literature offers various approaches for analyzing and evaluating the decentralization efforts of governments. For the purpose of this study, the public administration and finance approach seems most appropriate since it is primarily concerned with specific decisions about political processes, organizational structures, and fiscal resources, and it focuses inductively on micro analytical issues (Ascher 1987). However, in order to analyze decentralization efforts in a more directed manner, it is important from the outset to distinguish among different types and degrees of decentralization.

Rondinelli (1990) characterizes four types of decentralization. The first is political decentralization, which aims to give more political power for decision making to citizens or to their elected representatives and is usually associated with citizen participation and democratization. Determining how best to achieve political decentralization and assessing the actual extent of this transfer of power must be considered in the specific political context of a society. The second type of decentralization is spatial decentralization. In this case governments seek to achieve a more balanced pattern of urban development and to prevent or reverse high levels of concentration in certain metropolitan areas through strengthening and promoting economic development in the less developed areas. This form is closely linked to the third type of decentralization, administrative decentralization, in the sense that these two forms are mutually reinforcing.

Administrative decentralization can be defined as:

> the transfer of responsibility for planning, management, and the raising and allocation of funding from the central government and its agencies to field units of government, agencies, subordinate units or levels of government, semi-autonomous public authorities or corporations, regional or functional authorities, or non-governmental organizations (Rondinelli and Nellis 1986: 5).

There are three forms of administrative decentralization which outline the different possible degrees of achievement. Deconcentration is the weakest form and usually the first step of highly centralized governments in the process of decentralization. Deconcentration refers to the redistribution of decision-making authority and financial and management responsibilities among different levels within the central government. A common instrument is the creation of field offices, as was the case in Mexico under the Decentralization Program of Federal Public Administration in 1985 (V. Rodríguez 1992: 133). Through delegation, the second aspect of administrative decentralization, "central ministries transfer responsibility for decision-making and administration to semi-autonomous organizations not wholly controlled by the central government but ultimately accountable to it" (Rondinelli 1990: 11). Devolution is the last step and politically the most important, because it involves the granting of autonomy, the right to generate revenues, and the authority to make spending decisions to the local, municipal level (Sherwood 1969).[1]

---

[1] Interestingly, in Spanish there is no word that effectively encompasses the meaning of devolution. *Devolver* comes closest, but this suggests giving something back; it is less than precise in this particular case, given that we are speaking of something that was never enjoyed or obtained in the first place.

The fourth type of decentralization is economic decentralization. Liberalizing economies often attempt to transfer power away from the center by decentralizing in this way. Economic decentralization can take a number of forms, such as different types of privatization (e.g., contracting out) and various forms of public-private partnerships (Rondinelli 1990:11 ff).

The Practice: Decentralization in Mexico

While the theoretical framework discussed above is useful, in practice decentralization is not so neatly categorized, and efforts to decentralize must be analyzed within the country's specific political and social context. In the case of the Mexican political system, the centralization of political and economic decision-making power at the federal level and the enormous power vested in the president have had a significant influence on the country's decentralization efforts.

From the 1970s onward, there was increasing pressure for opening in the Mexican political system (partially offset by the reforms of 1973 and 1977). The country's economic collapse in 1982, coupled with the political crisis, shook the nation's faith in its presidentialist and centralist system's ability to respond to national needs. Thus, both politically and developmentally, from 1983 onward the commitment to decentralize began to quicken (V. Rodríguez 1987).

President de la Madrid held power during the early phase of political opening, and the legacy of his presidency is significant to the continuing effort to decentralize political and economic decision-making power. His first explicit commitment to decentralization appeared in Mexico's 1983–1988 national development plan, which defined three goals of decentralization: to strengthen federalism, to promote regional development, and to fortify the municipalities (V. Rodríguez 1992: 131 ff). The principal legislative instrument for implementing this plan was the individual development agreement (*convenio único de desarrollo*, CUD), which promoted regional development and also included funding for education and health. Through these regional development agreements, the central government formally transferred federal resources to the states as a means of achieving a greater level of genuine federalism.

But the cornerstone of all de la Madrid's decentralization efforts was the 1984 municipal reform, which amended Article 115 of the constitution and created the legal basis for increasing the municipal autonomy already guaranteed in the constitution. The key amendments give the municipalities autonomy in managing their finances and in designing their own rules of governance (Section II); define which services the municipalities must provide (Section III); and grant municipal governments all revenues collected through property taxation and the provision of public services (Section IV) (V. Rodríguez 1992).

Despite these efforts, decentralization during the de la Madrid administration shifted a share of power from the federal to the state level only, not all the way down to the municipality (V. Rodríguez 1987). Municipalities remained heavily dependent upon higher levels of government, especially the state, which was the conduit through which any decentralized resources would be transferred to the local arena (V. Rodríguez 1992: 137). The failure to devolve sufficient fiscal resources and infrastructure to the municipalities constrained their efforts to become more autonomous.

Of course, this was partly a result of state governors wanting to hold on to the resources themselves, and it also reflected PRI and governmental orthodoxy, whereby municipal presidents depended upon their governors for patronage, direction, and resources (Graham 1971; Fagen and Tuohy 1972). Therefore, it was not PRIísta municipal presidents who first began to press for these newfound rights and responsibilities, since this would have brought them into conflict with PRI governors. Rather, it was PANista municipal presidents like Francisco Barrio and Luis Alvarez in Ciudad Juárez and Chihuahua City, respectively, who first insisted upon local implementation of the reformed Article 115. They were not bound by party loyalty to the state authorities, but they were vulnerable in that they relied upon some state and federal subventions which, they feared, could be withheld for partisan reasons (Rodríguez and Ward 1992; V. Rodríguez 1995).

Thus, although de la Madrid's municipal reform did not bring a real transfer of power to most municipalities, it did shift the locus of primary control over municipalities from the federal to the state level. More importantly, this reform laid the groundwork for future efforts to decentralize. Actions to strengthen municipalities, especially the revisions to Article 115, created a solid framework within which the process of decentralization might continue; by the late 1980s, decentralization had become a primary element in political discourse.

When Carlos Salinas assumed the presidency in 1988, he continued and furthered the policy of the preceding administration. However, Salinas's decentralization agenda differed from de la Madrid's in two important respects. First, the decentralization efforts under de la Madrid can be characterized as largely *vertical* since the redistribution of power was intended primarily to strengthen the lower levels of government. The Salinas administration's approach tended more toward *horizontal* decentralization in that the redistribution of power extended to opposition parties as well. Second, the financial mechanism through which Salinas most frequently channeled resources to the periphery is PRONASOL, which, while heavily decentralized in outcomes and community participation, is nevertheless heavily centralized in terms of overall control and direction (V. Rodríguez 1993).

While PRONASOL was designed primarily as an antipoverty program, it also serves the goal of decentralization. Of PRONASOL's three main objectives—better living conditions for the poor, balanced regional development, and increased local and private participation—the last two lead toward decentralization. Because federal funding for PRONASOL projects goes directly to local groups and communities which can allocate the funds as they see fit, PRONASOL contributes to the autonomy of these groups and, to the extent that the municipality is involved, to the municipality's autonomy as well (V. Rodríguez 1993). Bypassing the state governments in this manner impedes the centralization of power at the state level. However, PRONASOL also operates in ways that increase the importance of the federal government and the power of the presidency. Viewed from this perspective, Salinas and PRONASOL may actually have centralized rather than devolved power (Bailey 1994).

Democratization through Decentralization: Baja California

If the actual transfer of power to states and municipalities was characterized by some ambivalence on the part of President Salinas and the PRI, the PAN was eager to embrace the new-found opportunities—at least at the municipal level prior to 1989 (Rodríguez and Ward 1992). Once Baja California came under the PAN's control, however, it remained to be seen how far a PANista state governor would actively encourage the devolution of power and whether he would treat PRI and PAN municipalities alike. Intergovernmental relations suddenly took an interesting turn as the stranglehold that the PRI traditionally exercised upon the state government was broken, first in Baja California and later in Guanajuato and Chihuahua. In each case, the incoming governor had previously been the municipal president of a major city (Ruffo of Ensenada, Medina Plascencia of León, and Barrio of Ciudad Juárez) and had experienced the pressures and constraints imposed by higher levels of fiscal and political authority.

The PAN's 1985 platform included the following: "the free municipality should have economic autonomy and political freedom; *the road to democracy surely must run through the free municipality*" (PAN 1985: 9, emphasis added). As described in chapter 2, over the decade of the 1980s Baja California experienced steady increases in both its overall and its urban population and, concomitantly, an increased demand for water and sewerage services, acceptable housing, reliable transportation systems, and education and health services. The growth of urban problems in Baja California's municipalities underscored the need for effective, efficient public administration, and this situation provided the first

PANista administration with the opportunity to experiment and to test the boundaries of municipal reform and decentralization.

During the 1986–1989 triennium in Ensenada, municipal president Ernesto Ruffo took up the idea of efficient administration and sought to apply its principles to address the needs of the municipality. He pressed the state government for more leeway and more money to work on Ensenada's problems. Ruffo argued that without more administrative and fiscal autonomy, he could do little for his municipality. In part, at least, it appears that these efforts were frustrated by a state government unwilling to relinquish control. Running for state governor in 1989, Ruffo campaigned on a platform that emphasized greater municipal autonomy and greater efficiency in administration, echoing the state PAN's view that, in order to increase both efficacy and autonomy, the municipality should be strengthened economically and politically (PAN 1989).

In 1989, Ruffo brought to the governorship a desire to decentralize, based both on his experience as a municipal president seeking autonomy and on his belief in the right of self-governance (interview with Ruffo, March 12, 1993). The various plans, programs, and agreements of his administration provide clear evidence of a genuine political will to take the actions necessary to decentralize effectively, such as implementing Article 115 in a meaningful way. The state's 1990–1995 development plan postulates that, although a centralized political system was once necessary "because factionalizing and breaking the links between the country's center and its regions would have blocked the emergence of national unity and a national identity," such a centralized system is no longer effective. Indeed, the rationale for decentralizing is based primarily on an economic development argument (PAN 1985: 15). The way to go about strengthening the federal system is to strengthen the municipality by increasing its administrative and fiscal autonomy (PAN 1985: 11), given that the municipality is closest to the needs of the community. However, the 1990–1995 development plan also acknowledges that municipal technical and administrative structures must be modernized before they can be fully capable of carrying out their responsibilities. Consequently, the state must encourage and support the modernization of the municipalities through a coordinated program of decentralization, whereby the state transfers "the goods and services that will strengthen the municipalities' capacity to address the urgent priorities which their communities confront" (PAN 1985: 122). According to the development plan, Article 115 and various cooperative agreements provide the framework within which the process of decentralization will take place.

The Decentralization Program to Strengthen Municipalities reiterates the state government's commitment to increase municipal autonomy. It explains in detail the objectives of decentralizing, emphasizing the importance of an ordered and gradual transfer of responsibilities and finances. The program also expresses the state's willingness to go beyond minimal legal requirements in granting autonomy to the municipalities. The key areas of responsibility that must by law be transferred from the state to the municipalities include property assessment, the issuance of building permits, urban planning, traffic control, and provision of water services. While the state is not required to transfer less critical functions (such as public investment and the administration of recreational and cultural programs and facilities), many of these are seen to fall naturally within the province of the municipal governments and may be transferred as well. What specific functions will be transferred, along with the scheduling of the transfers, are to be negotiated between the state and the individual municipalities through collaborative agreements that cover both mandatory transfers and negotiated rights and responsibilities (Baja California 1990).

Baja California's commitment to decentralize is reflected in the various types of transfers that have occurred at the state and local levels. Deconcentration was undertaken through the transfer of responsibility for the construction, maintenance, and conservation of potable water facilities from the federal Ministry of Public Works to the State Commission for Public Services. The ministry's responsibility to construct and maintain rural roads was transferred to the Development Agency for Rural Communities, and the task of building and upgrading schools is now in the hands of the Office for State Development (Promotora Estatal). The regularization of commonly held (*ejido*) land was transferred to the Baja California Commission for the Regularization of Land Tenure. These initiatives provided the mechanisms whereby federal government controls were restructured to give the state some real autonomy in its day-to-day operations.

The transfer of property assessments from the state to the municipal level, first in Mexicali and later in the other three municipalities, gives municipalities an important source of revenue, as well as the authority to manage this self-generated income. The rationalization of the tax system and the computerization of administrative infrastructure were important improvements which allowed municipalities to collect taxes more efficiently. Some of these self-generated revenues are to be used to cover the costs of the duties newly transferred to the municipalities. Decentralization agreements were also reached in the areas of culture and sports, transportation, and liquor licensing.

The exercise of municipal autonomy extends to reviewing whether certain functions might best be carried out by private rather than public providers. Ensenada municipal president Jesús del Palacio stated that the private sector should take over those tasks that the public sector cannot provide as efficiently, including, perhaps, property assessment and the operation of the municipal slaughterhouse and government daycare centers (interview with del Palacio).

These examples demonstrate that decentralization has occurred, to various degrees, in many areas in Baja California. While in and of itself this does not imply intent on the part of the state government to relinquish political and economic power, there are three distinguishing features in Baja California's decentralization program which suggest that the intent might be genuine. First, the responsibilities being passed to the municipal level include areas of importance to the future development of the entire state. For example, decisions about infrastructure and education and health services now fall to the municipalities. If the state did not intend to share some of its power with lower levels of government, it certainly would reserve such crucial areas to itself. Second, the Ruffo administration's encouragement of checks and balances among the three branches of state government (discussed in chapter 4) indicates a willingness to share or surrender some of the power traditionally concentrated in the executive branch. This willingness lends credence to the stated intent of increasing municipal autonomy. Third and possibly most important, the transfer of property assessment responsibility to the municipalities enables them to generate their own revenues and to spend those revenues as they see fit, offering a degree of municipal autonomy that would otherwise be impossible.

Decentralization in Practice: Follow the Money

In order to assess the extent and effectiveness of any decentralization program, and in particular the success of the Ruffo administration's initiatives, it is essential to examine the structure and administration of public finances. Legislation may make decentralization possible, but such a program gains political relevance only when the transfer of power (through deconcentration, delegation, or devolution) is accompanied by the fiscal resources and mechanisms that enable a particular government entity to exercise power.

The centralism that has traditionally characterized the Mexican political system extends to the financial realm. Resources have historically been concentrated at the federal level and, to a lesser degree, at the state level. In almost all cases, municipalities have had neither an adequate allocation of capital nor the ability to generate their own revenues in order to function as autonomous entities. Thus, in practice, municipal autonomy has often been beyond reach precisely because of a lack of resources (V. Rodríguez n.d.).

FISCAL COORDINATION AND REVENUE SHARING

State and local governments in Mexico currently obtain federal funds through two basic mechanisms. The first is regulated by the fiscal coordination law, reformed in 1990, which establishes that states are entitled to receive federal resources from two specific funds: the general fund and the municipal development fund. The amount of resources allocated to each state depends on a variety of factors, including a state's population, economic development, and contribution to the federal budget. Another provision of the fiscal coordination law stipulates that at least 20 percent of the general fund must be transferred to municipalities, although the law does not specify the portion that each is actually entitled to receive. The municipal development fund is turned over to the municipal authorities in its entirety (V. Rodríguez 1992).

The second mechanism is somewhat more discretionary and covers funding to state and local governments which comes from a variety of sources. One source is the individual development agreements signed annually between the federal government and each state (the CUDs) and their successors, the social development agreements. Additionally, state and local governments benefit from a variety of federally supported programs, such as PRONASOL. There are also projects such as the construction of highways, water treatment plants, dams, and so on, funded by the federal government under the category of special projects, which focus on areas of particular importance to individual communities. It is significant that funding received through this mechanism, although discretionary, is both substantial and important (V. Rodríguez n.d.).

The total of resources that state and local governments receive through these mechanisms determines the success of any effort to transfer power from higher to lower levels of government. It is precisely in this area of financial administration that Baja California has demonstrated considerable success. Evidence at both the state and local levels indicates that the upper tiers of government have directed more resources to lower levels and, more significantly, have ceded to these lower levels the authority and ability to generate and manage their own revenues.

REVENUE SHARING AND STATE FINANCES

An analysis of the structure and administration of Baja California's public finances reveals that from 1988 to 1991 there was an increase in federal contributions to the state. In 1988, the federal government contributed approximately U.S.$72.2 million; by 1991 this amount had increased to U.S.$185.4 million in real terms. There was also an increase in the resources that Baja California itself was able to collect. The data in figure 5.1 illustrate the dramatic increase in self-generated revenues, from approximately 45 billion pesos (U.S.$14 million) in 1988 to 123 billion pesos (U.S.$38.4 million) in 1991. The gain is due to increases in taxes (*impuestos*), fees (*derechos*), and fines and surcharges (*aprovechamientos*), which together offset the decrease in revenues collected on state property and other state assets (*productos*). (Taxes, fees, and fines/surcharges all increased by around 42 percent from 1988 to 1991, while

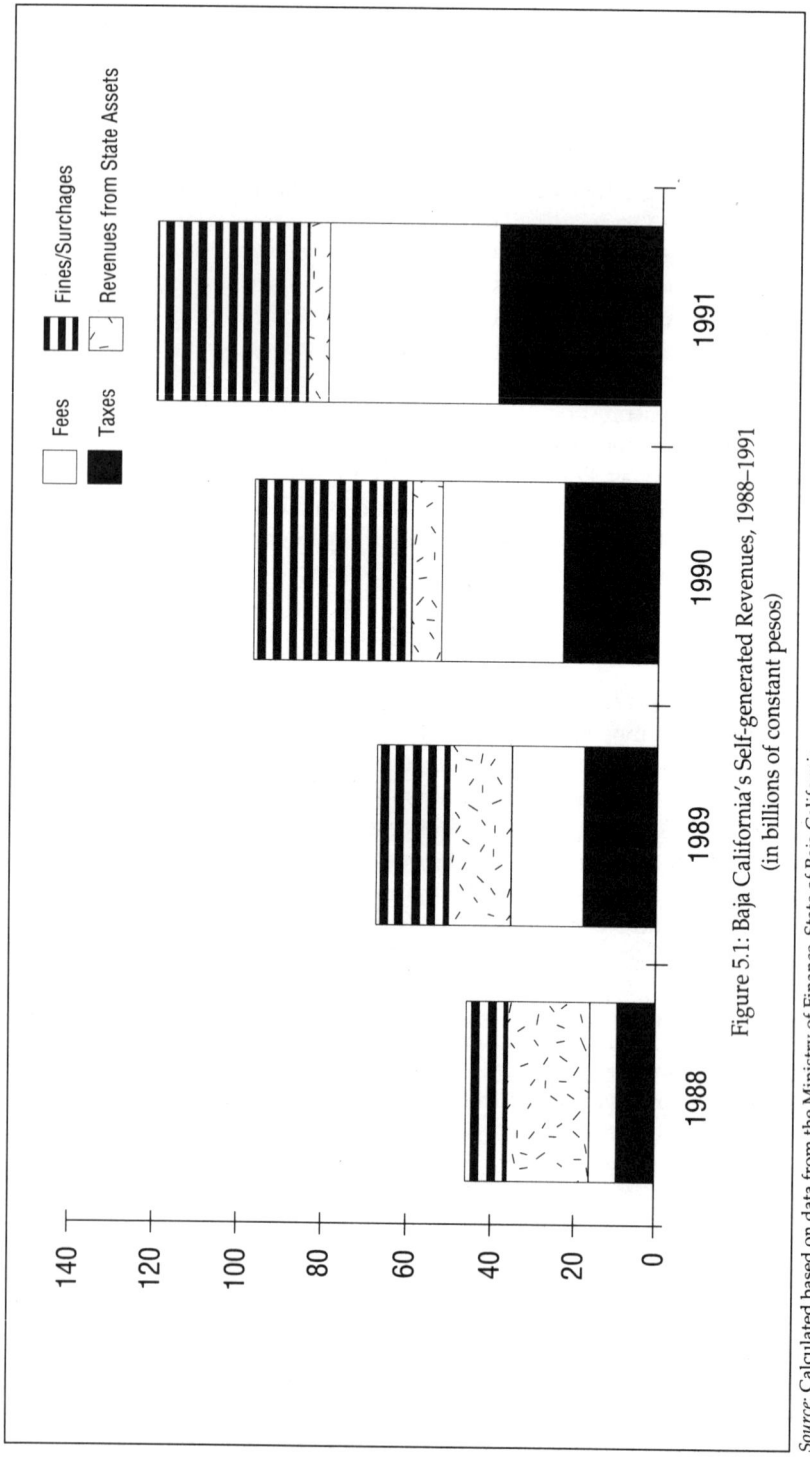

Figure 5.1: Baja California's Self-generated Revenues, 1988–1991 (in billions of constant pesos)

Source: Calculated based on data from the Ministry of Finance, State of Baja California

revenues from state assets declined by 24 percent.) The net increase in Baja California's resources is important, not only because it underscores the success of the decentralization efforts, but also because additional funding sources enhance the autonomy of the state government. More important than the increment in federal contributions, the boost in taxes, fees, and fines/surcharges collected by the Ruffo administration indicates that Baja California is gaining the ability to generate revenues independently of the federal government, thereby moving further down the path toward genuine decentralization.

The accumulation of additional state resources is not the only element changing in the relationship between the state of Baja California and the federal government. The fact that the Mexican constitution provides for the state and federal governments to divide up certain revenues between them created the potential for conflict between these levels of government over the administration of Mexico's value added tax (VAT). By law, 1.8 percent of this 4 percent tax may be retained by the federal government, and 2.2 percent by the state. Since 1990, according to the fiscal coordination law, the Ministry of Finance in Mexico City has control over all VAT income and sets its own criteria for returning some portion to the states. Although these criteria are formula-driven, the conflict over control of VAT revenues soured relations between the federal government and the Baja California state government throughout the Salinas administration.[2]

Governor Ruffo had signed the agreement that apportioned VAT income only after cutting a deal with the Ministry of Finance, under which Baja California was to receive federal appropriations equivalent to the sum that the state had contributed to the federal VAT pot. It does, in fact, appear that Baja California, like other wealthy states, is not receiving a fair share of the funds that it contributes to the federal government (interviews with Eugenio Elorduy Walther, January 11 and March 12, 1993). Although several governors have complained about this perceived unfair treatment, Ruffo's government was the first to openly challenge the Ministry of Finance over the perceived inequity, as well as the federal government's failure to return to the state its due under the fiscal coordination law.[3] The differences between Baja California and the PRI-governed states in this debate were

---

[2] The main reason for the reform of 1990 was that the total revenue from the VAT, which since 1983 had been collected by the states, had declined consistently. As tax evasion increased, VAT collection fell by 50 percent. Indeed, the revenue-sharing system had been reformed in 1983 precisely in order to transfer to the states the collection of the VAT. While collection at the local level generated great liquidity for the states, it had an adverse effect on the central government, mostly because the states would only send to Mexico City what they considered the federal government was entitled to receive. Inadvertently, a genuine system of decentralization had been created. The 1990 reform restituted the collection of the VAT to the federal government. Many states, particularly those with more efficient taxation systems, continuously demand that the collection of the VAT be returned to them (V. Rodríguez n.d.).

[3] State finance minister Elorduy Walther argued that Baja California receives about half the amount that it should; see also *Zeta*, May 8–14, 1992: 46A.

two: first, since Baja California controls the levying of the VAT, it knows how much is generated; second, the governor of Baja California has more liberty to challenge the president since he is not subject to the metaconstitutional rules discussed earlier (see chapter 4).

The mechanism for distributing federal appropriations, which returns less to the rich states than they contribute, penalizes Baja California. While the federal government claims the prerogative to redistribute some of the nation's wealth to the less advantaged states, Baja California's minister of finance, Elorduy Walther, claimed that the proportion was unjustifiably high and that it was actually in contravention of the VAT agreement that Ruffo (and all other governors) had signed with the federal Ministry of Finance. However, Ministry of Finance officials pointed out that, far from being penalized, Baja California had actually done better than other states. When negotiations between the state government officials and the representatives of federal agencies deadlocked in April 1993, Ruffo proposed that an independent arbitration group be created to resolve the conflict. The Ministries of Finance and the Interior concurred, and both sides turned over their data to the ad hoc arbitration group, which made a preliminary report in early June to the effect that the Ministry of Finance was, indeed, correct. The difference between the two positions appeared to rest on the number of enterprises upon which taxes are levied, with the state arguing that the ministry's list shows a 25 percent shortfall (Vicencio 1994). President Salinas asked the arbitration group to review the discrepancy between the two sides. The ministry's list was accepted as accurate, and the arbitration group reiterated its verdict that there was no case to answer. This represented a major defeat for Ruffo. In July 1993 he reported the decision to the state legislature, which proposed referring the matter to the Supreme Court. However, to date Ruffo has chosen not to pursue this option, probably because he believes that he will not win.

This case is very significant since it highlights the relative weakness of state finance ministries vis-à-vis the federal Ministry of Finance and the Office of the President. It also demonstrates how important it is for an opposition state government to maintain good working relations with the federal government—a lesson learned by Chihuahua governor Francisco Barrio, who ordered his finance minister to cooperate with the central authorities and to avoid the kind of difficulties that Elorduy Walther had created in Baja California. Our interviews with senior federal Ministry of Finance officials reveal that the Barrio administration's more compromising strategy produced better outcomes than the confrontational approach adopted by Baja California. The issue of more equitable revenue sharing with states and municipalities featured strongly in the recent presidential election campaign, and President Zedillo has pledged to increase the proportion of funds returned to the states and to intensify administrative decentralization efforts.

REVENUE SHARING AND MUNICIPAL FINANCES

The real test of decentralization's success lies in the municipalities' financial administration. As noted previously, local governments have historically been most constrained by the centralist tradition of the Mexican political system. Following the 1984 reform of Article 115, and especially since 1989, Baja California was able to implement changes to counter this centralization, and under Ruffo the state's three largest municipalities—Tijuana, Ensenada, and Mexicali—have been able to further strengthen their fiscal independence.

This situation is due largely to a series of bold actions taken by the Ruffo administration which capitalized on federal efforts to decentralize throughout the 1980s. Several additional factors also played a part. First, because there are only four municipalities in the state, decentralization has been relatively easy to implement (compared with states with large numbers of municipalities, though not necessarily large populations). Second, Tijuana, Ensenada, and Mexicali are economically prosperous and thus able to generate a substantial tax base. Third, opposition governments have recognized the need to take advantage of the possibilities opened up by current political projects to counteract centralization; greater competition in the political and electoral arenas forces municipal governments to take the initiative and assume responsibility in order to promote their agendas. Finally, human agency also intervened in Baja California's case. Ruffo's experience as a municipal president under siege gave him firsthand experience of how burdensome the constraints imposed by the state government could be. Perhaps even more important was Ruffo's strong belief that people work better and more productively when they are given responsibility, even if certain efficiencies are lost (interview with Ruffo, March 12, 1993).

By far the most important contributing factor in the increased autonomy of the Tijuana, Ensenada, and Mexicali governments was the Ruffo administration's decision to formalize the changing nature of public financial administration. An important step in solidifying the changes in the financial relationship between state and municipality was the signing of formal agreements to guide the transfer of responsibility for property assessment and taxation to the municipalities.[4] Ruffo went one step further; his first transfer of power was to the PRI-controlled municipality of Mexicali.

---

[4] Prior to the 1984 amendments to Article 115, property tax revenues went to the state, and even after the 1984 reform many state governments continued to collect property taxes on behalf of the municipalities, returning only a small proportion and keeping the rest as a "service charge" (V. Rodríguez 1987). And the contingencies that states sometimes imposed on even these returned monies left the municipality little oversight on their expenditure. Section IV of revised Article 115 gave municipalities the right to collect and retain all property tax revenue, and most states have amended their constitutions to implement this new provision (V. Rodríguez n.d.).

The agreements to transfer property assessment authority are crucial for various reasons. First, they actively involve the state in the devolution process. Second, because the state tailors the agreements on a case-by-case basis, municipalities that do not yet have the administrative infrastructure required for collecting property taxes can schedule the transfer to take this fact into account. Third, these agreements give the municipalities control over how the revenues are to be spent and the opportunity to plan expenditures more efficiently and for the longer term. This institutionalization is crucial since financial security is at the core of planning; it enables the municipalities to respond better to the demands of governance.

The municipalities' new areas of fiscal responsibility allowed them to realize a dramatic increase in self-generated revenues. This finding surfaced repeatedly in our fieldwork and is confirmed by financial records. Comparing the income side of the Mexicali budget during the administration of Milton Castellanos Gout (1989–1992) with that of his predecessor, Guillermo Aldrete Haas (1986–1989), is illustrative. In 1987 Mexicali collected 44 million constant pesos in taxes; in 1990, at the end of Castellanos Gout's second year in office, Mexicali took in 224 million pesos in real terms, for a 327 percent increase.

The increase in self-generated income is not limited to Mexicali. In Tijuana, the increase from 1987 to 1990 was 252 percent: tax revenues rose from 1.9 billion constant pesos in 1987 to 6.7 billion in 1990 and 9.1 billion in 1991, an overall increase of 380 percent over 1987 (see figure 5.2). Mexicali's municipal treasurer stressed the important role that this devolution played because it endowed the municipality with the financial means to achieve its goals (interview with Carlos Topete Noriega, January 15, 1993). More importantly, Topete Noriega stated that since the transfer of the property assessments registry in 1991, Mexicali has increased sevenfold the amount it collects in property taxes.

As Tijuana, Mexicali, and Ensenada have gained the power to collect property taxes, a new pattern has emerged in the composition of their municipal budgets. In the past, municipal budgets in Mexico traditionally had derived around 80 percent of their total revenues from federal and state appropriations, and only 20 percent from their own sources (even after the reform of Article 115). In an interview, former Ensenada municipal president Jesús del Palacio reported that by 1990, 55 percent of Ensenada's income was self-generated, with the remaining 45 percent coming through federal and state transfers. Other municipalities also experienced a diminishing reliance on extra-municipal sources because of their ability to generate their own revenues. In 1987, 60 percent of Mexicali's revenues were federal and state transfers, yet by 1991 this number had dropped to 48 percent. Tijuana had also reduced its dependence on outside funds to 38 percent of its budget by the 1990–1991 fiscal year (figure 5.3).

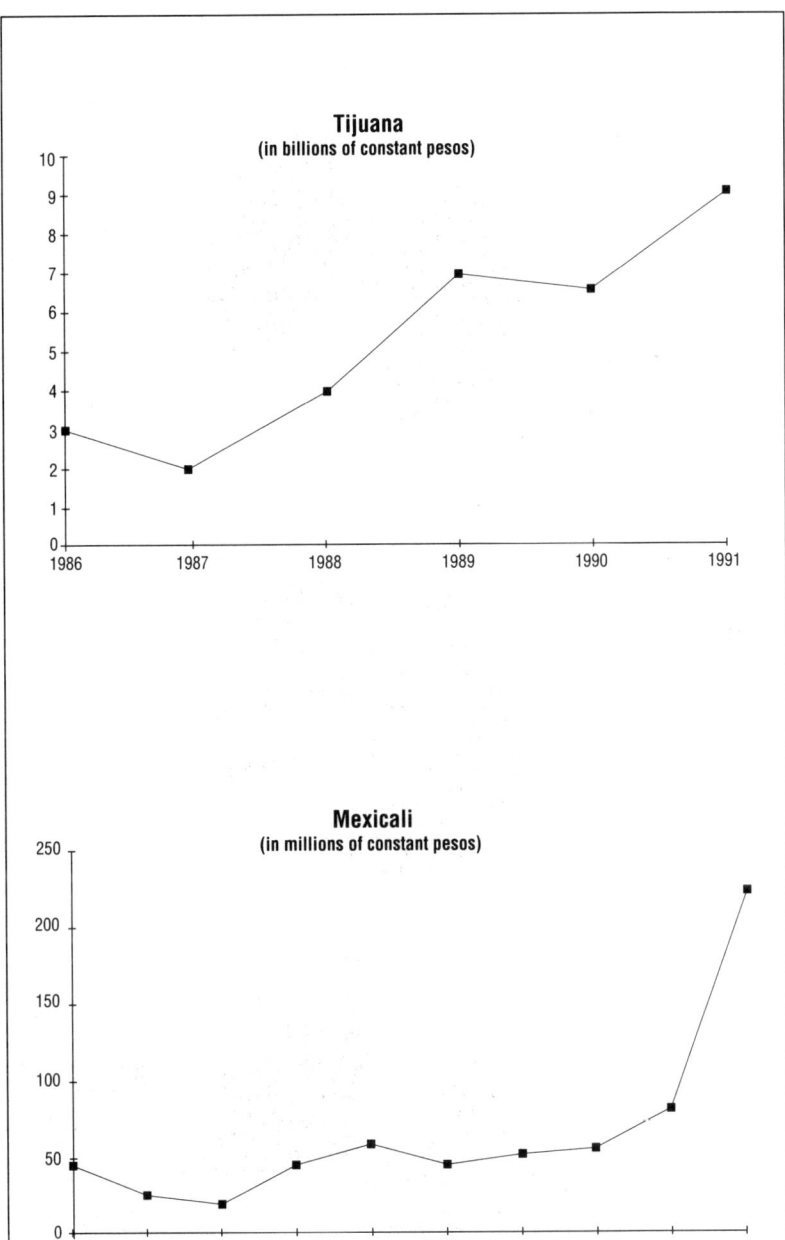

Figure 5.2: Tax Revenues Registered in Mexicali and Tijuana during the 1980s

Source: Calculated based on data from the Ministry of Finance, State of Baja California

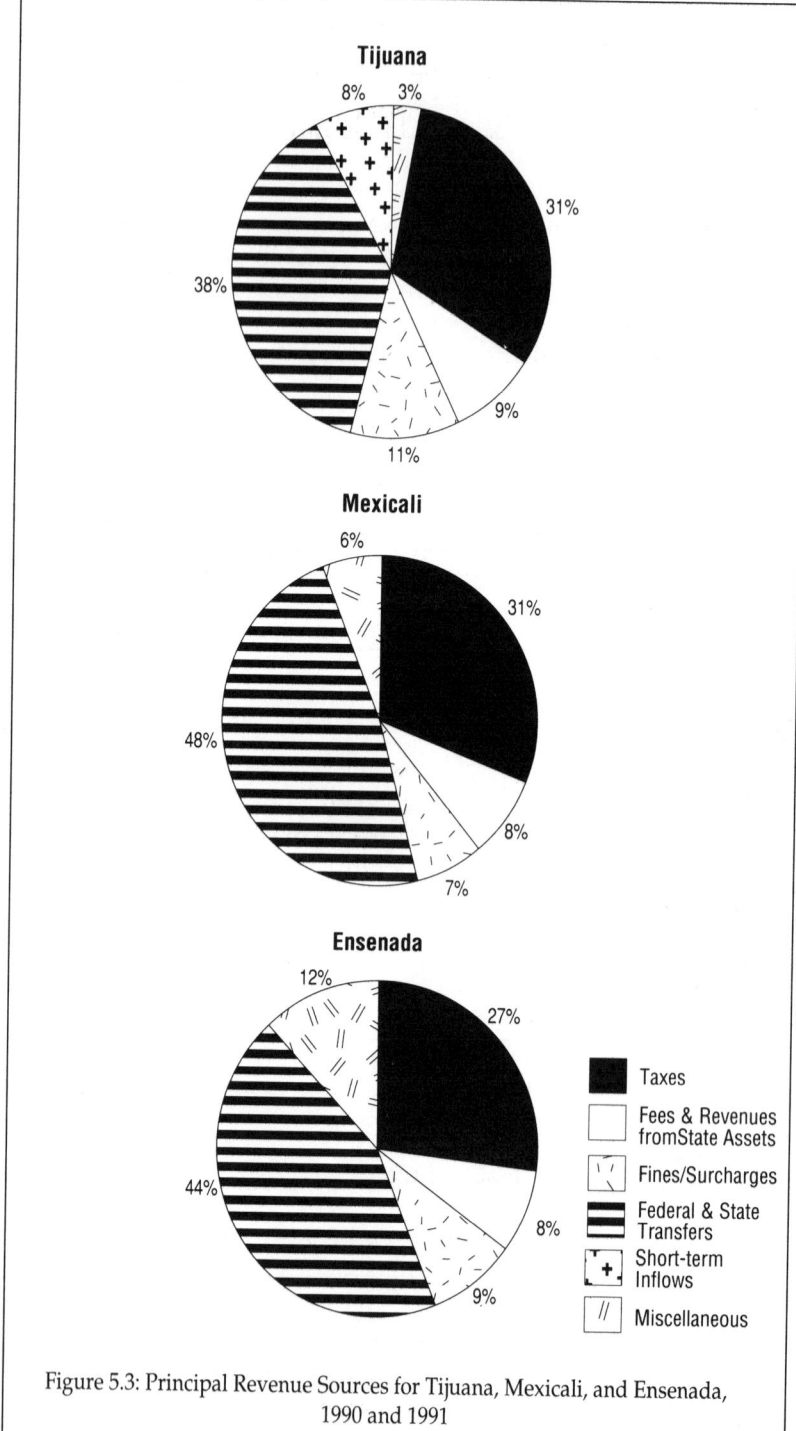

Figure 5.3: Principal Revenue Sources for Tijuana, Mexicali, and Ensenada, 1990 and 1991

Source: Calculated based on data from the Ministry of Finance, State of Baja California

The Relationship between Finance, Autonomy, and Power

The Ruffo administration's willingness to formalize the municipalities' control over public finances ensures their ability to generate more of their own revenues and decreases their reliance on funding from other levels of government, thereby increasing municipal autonomy and power. Ruffo's action is also significant because it opens the door to a different kind of relationship among the levels of government.

With increased economic independence, municipalities can adopt a new posture vis-à-vis the state government, and even openly challenge the state's authority. Municipalities now have more resources with which to provide services and implement policy agendas. In the political arena this independence became evident when Governor Ruffo reneged on his campaign promise to increase from 20 to 35 percent the amount that the state would transfer to municipalities from the general fund.[5] He was promptly and loudly attacked for this "breach of faith" by Mexicali municipal president Milton Castellanos Gout. What is interesting is that a PRI municipal president could openly challenge the governor (interview with Héctor Osuna Jaime, March 13, 1993).

Another way in which municipalities exercise increased autonomy from the state government is demonstrated by the fact that all four municipal presidents serving 1989–1992 terms applied directly to the federal government, sometimes to President Salinas himself, for funding for specific projects. This was especially true of Mexicali's Castellanos, who was criticized locally for spending excessive amounts of time in Mexico City in search of political and financial support. Some of the sought-after federal funding was certainly linked to PRONASOL. The fact that significant federal resources are channeled through this mechanism directly to the local communities, sidestepping the state governments, also suggests that the municipalities remain financially dependent on outside sources of funding. Although state government officials acknowledged that they were being bypassed by PRONASOL, they generally did not object to municipal presidents going directly to Mexico City for funds. A great portion of resources remain concentrated at the center, and allowing municipalities the freedom to contend for these resources appears to be consistent with Ruffo's decentralization of functions and powers.

Ruffo's commitment to transfer power and fiscal resources cuts across the board in Baja California. However, there have been allegations that Tijuana receives a disproportionate share of funds, particularly when compared with Mexicali, a municipality which is nearly as large in population. State officials have been quick to respond that the formula for state appropriations is based partly on population but also on a munici-

---

[5]Ruffo stated that he could not keep this promise because of the beleaguered condition of the state's finances and its inability to pay its bills, most notably in education.

pality's economic activity, and since agricultural activity (which accounts for a significant portion of Mexicali's income) is not taxable, Mexicali receives less in transferred funds per capita than Tijuana. Financial data corroborate that Mexicali was not treated substantially differently than the other municipalities simply because it was PRI-controlled.

Conclusion: Democratization through Genuine Decentralization

Governor Ruffo's initiatives prompted a new stage in the decentralization process via formalization of the financial policies and mechanisms that enable municipalities to increase their revenues and, ultimately, their autonomy. In our view, genuine decentralization is demonstrated through the meaningful transfer of power (usually reflected in the shifting composition of the municipal budgets) and the changing behavior of local governments vis-à-vis higher levels of government. This genuine recasting of intergovernmental relations, and the reduction of dependence upon higher levels of authority, have, we argue, created new opportunities for democracy and allowed self-government to emerge in practice. As described in the preceding chapter, both intra- and intergovernmental relations are structured in the constitution in ways that, in theory at least, are conducive to democratic development. Whether through the checks and balances embodied in the separation of powers or through federalist principles giving maximum power and freedom to the local level, the theory has not been implemented in practice. The opening of political space, economic liberalization, and a willingness on the part of the federal government and the president to surrender some share of power have allowed these principles to be applied in practice at the state level.

There is an apparent paradox associated with the new-found autonomy at the local level. Rather than being penalized and starved of resources by the federal government and PRI partisan concerns, PANista governments at the state and municipal levels have actually been less constrained than their PRI counterparts. Because they are not bound by PRI orthodoxy and career patronage, and because they recognize that they are unlikely to receive special favors, the PAN governments (and, to a lesser extent, PRD governments such as the one in Morelia, 1989–1992[6]) have found themselves able to exercise more autonomy, not less.[7] The important point for Baja California is the eventual outcome to be derived from this "paradox."

---

[6]The PRD potentially enjoys the same autonomy, but because it has been the target of attacks by Salinas and the PRI, municipal governance has been severely constrained; PRD city halls have been punished and starved of resources at every opportunity (Bruhn and Yanner 1995).

[7]Of course, this coin is two-sided: witness the greater freedom of maneuver that PRIísta municipal presidents in Mexicali have experienced now that they do not have to depend upon their party overlord, the governor, for approval of their agendas.

Ultimately it is the extent to which a real decentralization of functions and powers is achieved that will constitute Ruffo's democratization legacy. Changes in the electoral process, different patterns of recruitment and governance, the incipient separation of powers among the three branches of government, and extending decentralization—these developments mark a major change in the political landscape of Mexico. In the final chapter we address some of these new political traditions and assess the role played by both Ruffo and Salinas as architects of Mexico's new democracy.

6

Architects of Democracy? Changing Political Traditions in Mexico

Throughout this book we have argued a case for the quickening of democratization in Baja California. Obviously this process is not occurring in a vacuum; it is part of an overall change in the political traditions of Mexico guided by President Carlos Salinas. Hence our front cover to this monograph and the title of this chapter, suggesting that there are two principal architects of democracy in Baja California: former president Salinas, the architect of the broader context, and Governor Ruffo, the breakthrough victor, embodying an incipient institutionalization of democratic principles.

Constructing Democracy at the National Level

Looking back at the past *sexenio*, we feel that Salinas's achievements as an architect of the country's democratization process had only mixed success. Extending the metaphor, Salinas played a central role in tearing down some of the past monuments and shibboleths that both typified and reinforced the old authoritarian regime. Specifically, he curbed government-protected labor union gangsterism, opening up unions to more representative leadership. He removed incompetent governors, particularly those resistant to change or to the winning of elections by fair means rather than foul. He set in train internal reform of the PRI, began to dismantle and restructure its corporate base, and confronted the so-called dinosaurs and old-guard reactionaries in his party. The amendments to Article 27 to reform the *ejido* sector, which make possible the deregulation and privatization of communally held property, also increased the potential for greater pluralism and political competition in the countryside (Cornelius 1994).

Having cleared the site—or some parts of it—he went a long way to ensure that the new surface upon which to build is more level today than ever before. Notable achievements here were the passing and subsequent reforms of the COFIPE, offering, as they do, the opportunity for the most transparent and clean elections in Mexico's history. For the first time in over six decades the occupant of the presidency is no longer a foregone conclusion. Salinas also opened up new spaces in the political landscape by insisting on cleaner elections and respecting many opposition victories (especially those of the PAN), and by reversing some PRI gubernatorial and municipal victories where the conduct or outcome of an election was subject to dispute. The National Solidarity Program, too, has created new opportunities for greater civic participation in local development and has helped to restructure, and create new forms of, civic and political organization. NGOs continued to proliferate under Salinas, and many of these remain involved in furthering the democratization process and protecting gains made.[1]

But there were also some significant failures and setbacks. Elections are still far from squeaky clean; major irregularities were observed in the 1993 gubernatorial races in Coahuila and Yucatán, suggesting that some level of discretionality remains, undermining credibility in the overall system. Campaign spending thresholds, while they now exist, remain much higher than most parties except the PRI could ever hope to reach, and access to television for political and electoral purposes is still heavily stacked against non-PRI parties, as the August 21, 1994, elections clearly demonstrated (Ward et al. 1994). While those elections are generally considered to have represented a major advance in cleaning up the electoral process, questions remain over whether fraud might have had a significant effect in districts where the PRI won by a small margin and in the state elections in Chiapas. Moreover, now that the conduct of elections is more open and fair, attention has shifted to the systematic advantages that the PRI enjoys owing to its favored access to the media and its influence over major government spending programs such as PRONASOL and PROCAMPO, the argument being that these unfair advantages constitute today's mechanisms for perpetrating electoral fraud.

There was also little progress under Salinas in opening up the process of candidate selection within the PRI. The assassination of presidential candidate Luis Donaldo Colosio forced Salinas to engineer two *dedazos*, and a major power struggle appears to have taken place before he was able to impose Zedillo on the party over other candidates more in tune with the old guard. And the Zedillo imposition was not achieved without incurring a high cost: it appears to have tied Zedillo to

---

[1] Several coordinating organizations emerged during Salinas's administration, such as Convergencia, Movimiento Ciudadano Democrático, Acuerdo Nacional para la Democracia, and Alianza Cívica, among others.

Carlos Hank González's group—not one usually known for its zeal in the political reform arena. Nor was there any discernable difference from the old way of selecting PRI candidates for senatorial positions and deputyships, except that the lists were held back until the last possible moment in order to minimize the risk of disappointed candidates defecting to the PRD.

Another area where no progress was made is in the PRI's treatment of the PRD: one analyst conservatively estimates that there have been more than two hundred politically motivated murders of PRD militants since 1988. The Chiapas uprising has also drawn attention to the repression of civil rights in southern Mexico and to the military's alleged lack of respect for human rights in its attempts to quell the insurrection. Human rights legislation under Salinas failed to go beyond laws to protect individual rights through judicial process, and many states have yet to implement these measures.

A final caveat when proclaiming Salinas an architect of national democratization is the paradox that, in order to support this process, he was obliged to increase the powers of the presidency and reinforce presidentialism. Some analysts argue that a greater appropriation of power is necessary in order to push a reform program through (see, for example, Karl and Schmitter 1991: 252). Certainly many of the apparent breakthroughs in the democratization process in Mexico since 1988 occurred because they were introduced by presidential fiat. However, both centralization and an intensification of presidentialism may be viewed as impediments to reform (see Meyer 1989). Significantly, all three principal presidential candidates in 1994 called for a new federalism and for greater power and fiscal autonomy for the states. While Salinas was instrumental in making the breakthrough in democratization, the challenge of intensifying democratization and the devolution of power will fall to his successor. Much will depend on Zedillo's ability to create maneuvering space and on the extent to which he sees his electoral victory as a mandate for continuing the process of change.

Ruffo as Architect of Democracy in Baja California

Does Baja California stand out as an example of democratization "without adjectives," or does it, too, represent a case of constrained democratization? In order to begin to address this overarching question, let us first review some of the achievements of Ruffo's first years in office.

From the outset, there was change at the level of the state congress. In 1989, party pluralism transformed the congress into an arena of policy-shaping debate for the first time in the state's history. Although the PAN held nine of the nineteen legislative seats, it was often outvoted by alliances between PRI and PRD members, especially after Dolores de

Méndez abandoned the PAN to vote with the PRI. Thus, the 1989–1992 congress was rife with division, given to political positioning, and, most importantly, capable of challenging and even halting the governor's legislative initiatives. Forceful legislative action is perhaps most apparent in Ruffo's mixed results with electoral reform and his failure to obtain confirmation for many of his judicial appointees. In each of these cases, the congressional deputies checked the governor's intentions. Hence, Ruffo's early years offered a historic first: a Mexican governor facing willful and often successful opposition from a divided state legislature.

Whether or not this departure from the norm of PRI dominance and one-party rule represents a process of institutionalization is an open question. One indication that this may in fact be the case is the continuation of party rivalry into the 1992–1995 period. Another is the significant expansion of basic congressional supports (such as office space and facilities) and the initiation and strengthening of internal congressional commissions. Both of these steps suggest a continued empowerment of the legislative branch. Finally, competitive electoral patterns within the fifteen congressional districts of Baja California portend continued divisions within future congresses. In combination, these factors point toward vital and ongoing interaction between the legislative and executive spheres.

In another break with traditional forms of executive dominance, Ruffo has empowered the judicial branch on two counts. One of these is Ruffo's insistence that members of the judiciary select their own president, as is required by law. Second, Ruffo endorsed the creation of the Office of the State Attorney General for Human Rights and did so before President Salinas took a similar federal initiative. Significantly, the Baja California office and the associated Human Rights Commission will be under congressional oversight and therefore independent of the executive branch, at least to the extent that the congress itself is an independent agent. The commission is charged with ensuring respect for human rights at the state level, as these are defined in the Mexican constitution and in the Universal Declaration of Human Rights—a demand heard throughout Mexico.

Beyond intrastate relations, chapters 4 and 5 signal the advanced degree of autonomy achieved by municipal governments vis-à-vis the state authorities. Indeed, contrary to the expectations of many observers, Baja California displays a substantial rise in municipal-level independence. Such independence is manifested in a number of municipal inroads made upon traditional state authority. Here we recall two. On the one hand, Ruffo has actively pursued the transfer of numerous state responsibilities to the municipalities. Granted, in most cases these responsibilities were legally the charge of the municipal governments in the first place, but this is exactly the point: PRI governors had never been disposed to devolve any but the most remedial and insignificant powers to municipal governments. On the other hand, Ruffo has gone beyond merely eschewing a state monopoly of municipal consigns. He has eagerly endorsed the municipalities' drive for greater control over and collection of their own fiscal resources. As indicated in chapter 5, the most significant step in this direction has been the transfer of the property assessment registry and the associated opportunities to collect property taxes. This transfer alone sets Baja California on the track of real decentralization. Interestingly, the PRI-led Mexicali administration—the "opposition's opposition"—was the first municipality to obtain the transfer of property assessment and subsequently the most successful in multiplying many times over its income from property taxes. In short, the Ruffo administration has devolved to municipal governments unheard-of powers and responsibilities which, arguably, undercut the state government's control over decisions and processes affecting the development of the entire state. While such transfers may well be argued on the basis of efficiency and sound administrative practice, they nevertheless go hard against Mexico's top-down political traditions.

Finally, and pointing back toward our overriding question, we turn to state-federal relations. The essential element here is the relatively congenial relationship that Ruffo enjoyed with Salinas, although it was not quite so cozy as Francisco Barrio's relations with the federal government and the president (for which he has been criticized). Indeed, the Salinas administration appeared to learn an important lesson from Baja California, for many analysts argue that Ruffo's statewide electoral success followed from his poor treatment as Ensenada's mayor by then PRI governor Xicoténcatl Leyva. While Leyva was withholding funds from then mayor Ruffo, he was simultaneously gaining such a reputation for mismanagement that Salinas had to demand his resignation. Ruffo, a capable populist, paved his way to the governor's mansion by sweeping the walkway in front of city hall, the quintessential symbol of changes both needed and to come.

Once in the governor's mansion, Ruffo received Salinas's endorsement, and the federal government promised Baja California its share of national and PRONASOL funds. However, the state government seems to have stepped over the line when Ruffo criticized the federal Ministry of Finance's formula for allocating funds to the state and pressed for a higher level of revenue sharing. His challenge was rebuffed. It is also noteworthy that Salinas refrained from intervening in Ruffo's transfer of power to the municipalities. Indeed, Salinas appears to have supported such devolution.

Full Democracy or Partial Political Liberalization?

Is Mexico witnessing the initial stages of a truly democratic unfolding in its border zone, with Baja California and Chihuahua serving, as one popular title puts it, as "laboratories of democracy"?[2] Moreover, who is the architect of Baja California's democracy? Was it Ruffo, the governor and victor? Or did Salinas mastermind Baja California's political opening in order to legitimate and prolong the PRI's hold on power nationally?

A definitive response to these questions is elusive and made especially problematic by the analytical perspective taken—either regional or national. Placing Baja California in national perspective, some observers have speculated that this state's unfolding democracy is only part of a larger PRI strategy designed to claim wider legitimacy for the national political system. In this view, the loose leash that Salinas granted Ruffo represents another instance of the PRI government's intent to shape democracy through strategic interventions. Particularly where such interventions were fashioned as noninterventions—as seems to have been the case in Baja California—Salinas was at his best as an architect of democracy. It is unclear, however, whether Salinas deliberately set the stage for Ruffo's victory by designating as the PRI contender in the 1989 gubernatorial race a woman who would be unlikely to capture the imagination of the statewide electorate. In this vein, the PAN's victory in Baja California may be viewed with as much skepticism as any gubernatorial victory in Mexico. At its worst, it can be seen as a mere token concession to the ultimate objective of stabilizing the political system.

Skepticism about the political process in Baja California also emerges among analysts with a distinctly regional focus, who find only a limited transformation of PRI-society relations. The PRI is making a concerted effort to refurbish its links to civil society, especially through the Urban Popular Territorial Movement, whose enthusiastic young leaders and staffers are committed to a more democratic PRI. The movement gives priority to the bottom-up channeling of neighborhood concerns, but it remains to be seen whether it can prevent entrenched PRI militants from monopolizing the organization for their own ends (Hernández Rodríguez 1991: 227 ff). Also in doubt is the PRI's ability to reshape its relations with old-style corporate structures (Guillén López 1993).

The PAN, meanwhile, faces numerous dilemmas of its own, not least of which regards its party base. Having started its 1989 campaign with an official membership of minimal proportions, the PAN has not significantly developed its local membership. Indeed, the party leadership appears to have abandoned any strategy to secure the party bases. Far from working to expand its membership base, it continues to impose strict conditions for

---

[2]The context of David Osborne's (1988) *Laboratories of Democracy* is admittedly very different, but the parallel notion holds of states serving as arenas of experimentation within the larger national setting.

party membership. As a result, the PAN is forced to rely upon good governance as the sole basis of its appeal to an unsecured electorate. And while Ruffo readily embraces this good governance yardstick as the key to future electoral success, the volatile electoral trends that we have witnessed make this a high-risk strategy. Ironically, the good governance appeal might eventually backfire, especially if the PRI, with its substantial party base, succeeds in convincing the electorate that it, too, is capable of governing effectively—as it is doing in Mexicali. The PAN also faces continuing divisions within its ranks, as longtime *magallones* continue to take issue with the pragmatic politics of the neoPANistas. And finally, the thinness of the PAN's ranks presents an ongoing problem for candidate recruitment and for the identification of qualified, experienced leadership, as discussed in chapter 3.

At the other end of the political spectrum, the PRD has shown extreme vulnerability at the polls, winning a plurality in the 1988 presidential contest but being virtually eclipsed in the 1989 elections. Although the PRD was awarded all four at-large seats in the state legislature, the party's efforts to augment its base appear to be undermined by the fact that its natural constituents—many of the state's popular organizations—have adopted a highly pragmatic, nonpartisan position. Indeed, the PRD's electoral prospects appear poor when we recall that this "party of the people" won a mere 3 percent of the vote in the 1992 congressional elections.[3]

Lacking a solid base, opposition parties in Baja California may well be vulnerable. If the PRI were to reassert itself through fair electoral gains—a real possibility—or through some form of electoral manipulation—which appears less likely, given electoral reforms—this would have significant implications for many of the democratization processes that we have discussed. For instance, a resurgent PRI could potentially diminish the now high levels of contestation found in the state legislature, and it might well reestablish the predominance of the executive branch vis-à-vis the legislature and judiciary. Furthermore, the many administrative and budgetary changes under way, which promise so much for municipal administrative efficiency, need not serve the ends of democratization per se. Rather, if these were adopted by PRI governments, they might serve to give the PRI a modernizing face-lift and provide legitimation without full democratization.[4] The fact is that the PRI has acknowledged the need for, and initiated, the aforementioned aspects of internal restructuring that could potentially revive its underlying structure and raison d'être, thus giving it still further

---

[3]Earlier in this monograph we went so far as to cast doubt upon the legitimacy of such a small plurality having such a significant representation in congress (four of the nineteen seats).

[4]Certainly it appears that PRIísta municipal governments do improve their administrative records and adopt many of the practices and reforms implemented by their PANista predecessors. See, for example, the PRIísta Ciudad Juárez case under Jaime Bermúdez, which retained many of the innovations introduced by Francisco Barrio (Rodríguez and Ward 1992; Ordóñez Barba 1991).

advantages over the PAN and other national opposition parties. Should the PRI even partly realize these aims, the context may shift dramatically in its favor. Indeed, we predict that if the PRI wins back the state in 1995, this will pose enormous problems to an ousted PAN. How could the PAN, having lost to the PRI after campaigning on a good governance platform, begin to recoup such a loss without a significant party base?[5]

At worst, the cumulative weight of the preceding observations points to a dire conclusion: changes to date may serve to liberalize the politics of Baja California—for instance, delivering elements of citizen rights and purging government of its most blatant abuses—without in fact delivering democracy. Nevertheless, we believe that we are observing the emergence of a genuine process of democratization. Several additional features of Baja California's society, geography, and economy are important here, not least its status as a border region of marked socioeconomic diversity. This is an area distinguished by relatively high levels of income and education, and by the pressures of a large and fluid immigrant population. Baja California has also felt the impact of elite ruptures, shattering the bonds that traditionally tied industrial elements to the PRI.[6] These business-oriented groups and individuals are geared toward economic progress, and they are less than convinced that the PRI—especially in its traditional form—is a better means to that end than the current PAN. The various popular organizations with which we came in contact expressed continued frustration with the inaccessibility of the PRI, and the bulk of the electorate has turned a deaf ear to this party, whose image has been sullied by allegations of corruption under the last two PRI governors.

Thus, despite the PAN's structural weakness as a party and the PRD's even greater vulnerability, the PRI's electoral prospects appear to be shaky. Yet a caveat is in order: the PRI remains an electoral force of substance. We conclude, therefore, that political competition, not PANista dominance, is the defining characteristic of Baja California's recent political experience. Provided that this trend is not thrown into reverse, we have the basis for a genuinely democratic polity. Even if the PRI were to regain its former dominance of state-level politics, such a reversal need not annul the important changes seen in the transfer of powers from state to municipal levels. We are inclined to believe that administrative changes, underscored by the rationalization of Baja California's municipal governments and their more dynamic role in assessing the

---

[5] In such a scenario they would be almost entirely dependent upon the PRI performing very badly in government. This is hardly likely, given the reforms undertaken nationally and the PRI's bitter experience of being sidelined locally.

[6] Guillén López (1993) argues that elite ruptures were crucial in making electoral competition viable in Baja California. We also saw such ruptures in the pragmatic, nonpartisan positioning of various business groups and individuals whom we interviewed.

needs of their communities, promise to vitalize local politics and political debate, whichever party is in power. Accessibility, communication, and public interest all seem likely to increase as local administrations take a more active role in the lives of the citizenry, and vice versa. Ten years of active opposition governments, and many more years of oppositional electoral competition, appear to have made headway in restructuring Baja California's political culture.

Finally, we may reflect on the spillover effect that the Baja California experience has had upon the wider democratization process in Mexico. Obviously, one cannot underestimate the significance of the victory itself. Against a backcloth of several opposition gubernatorial victories that many analysts believe occurred but were denied through the manipulation of electoral results, the Baja California victory symbolized a sea change. It signaled to the international community that Mexico was committed to democratic change, and it helped to remove some of the tarnish left by the 1988 presidential election. Most important of all, it extended party pluralism from the legislative branch to executive government, though not yet at the federal level. Once the possibility of a non-PRI state government was demonstrated, this opened a window of opportunity for the PAN to triumph in Chihuahua in 1992. Further, the reforms undertaken in Baja California's electoral arena have led to national changes which most observers believe are conducive to wider democratization. Others argue that these reforms were already on-line and that their introduction in Baja California is unimportant. Perhaps so, but in our view their active and advanced implementation made the national process inevitable. We would expect, also, that the conditions of democratization which we have described—decentralization, greater municipal autonomy, the separation of powers, local community-group empowerment, and so on—might have a wider national spin-off and contribute to changing Mexico's political traditions.

Acronyms

CEE	Comisión Electoral Estatal/State Electoral Commission
CNC	Confederación Nacional Campesina/National Peasants' Confederation
CNOP	Confederación Nacional de Organizaciones Populares/National Confederation of Popular Organizations
COCUTAC	Comité de Colonias Urbanas de Tijuana, Asociación Civil/Committee of Urban Neighborhoods of Tijuana
COFIPE	Código Federal de Instituciones y Procedimientos Electorales/Federal Code of Electoral Institutions and Procedures
CROC	Confederación Revolucionaria de Obreros y Campesinos/Revolutionary Confederation of Workers and Peasants
CROM	Confederación Regional Obrera Mexicana/Regional Confederation of Mexican Workers
CRT	Confederación Revolucionaria de Trabajadores/Revolutionary Confederation of Workers
CTM	Confederación de Trabajadores de México/Confederation of Mexican Workers
CUD	Convenio Unico de Desarrollo/Individual Development Agreement
EAP	Economically active population
FDN	Frente Democrático Nacional/National Democratic Front
FONATUR	Fondo Nacional de Fomento al Turismo/National Tourism Development Fund
IFE	Instituto Federal Electoral/Federal Electoral Institute

ISSTECALI	Instituto de Seguridad y Servicios Sociales de los Trabajadores del Estado–Baja California/Social Security Institute for State Workers–Baja California
ITAM	Instituto Tecnológico Autónomo de México/ Autonomous Technological Institute of Mexico
ITESM	Instituto Tecnológico y de Estudios Superiores de Monterrey/Monterrey Technological Institute
LOPPE	Ley Federal de Organizaciones Políticas y Procesos Electorales/Federal Law of Political Organizations and Electoral Processes
NGOs	Nongovernmental organizations
PAN	Partido Acción National/National Action Party
PARM	Partido Auténtico de la Revolución Mexicana/Authentic Party of the Mexican Revolution
PCM	Partido Comunista Mexicano/Mexican Communist Party
PDH	Procuraduría de los Derechos Humanos/Office of the State Attorney General for Human Rights
PDM	Partido Demócrata Mexicano/Mexican Democratic Party
PEMEX	Petróleos Mexicanos
PFCRN	Partido del Frente Cardenista de Reconstrucción Nacional/Party of the Cardenista Front for National Reconstruction
PPS	Partido Popular Socialista/Socialist Popular Party
PRD	Partido de la Revolución Democrática/Party of the Democratic Revolution
PRI	Partido Revolucionario Institucional/Institutional Revolutionary Party
PRONASOL	Programa Nacional de Solidaridad/National Solidarity Program
PST	Partido Socialista de los Trabajadores/Socialist Workers' Party
SNTE	Sindicato Nacional de Trabajadores de la Educación/ National Union of Education Workers
UNAM	Universidad Nacional Autónoma de México/National University of Mexico
UNE	Unión Nacional de Enlace/National Union for Citizen Linkage

References

Aguilar Camín, Héctor, and Lorenzo Meyer. 1993. *In the Shadow of the Mexican Revolution: Contemporary Mexican History, 1910–89.* Austin: University of Texas Press.
Alcocer V., Jorge. 1994. "Cambios en el sistema," *Proceso* 918 (June 6): 47–48.
Alvarez, José Rogelio. 1989. *Diccionario Enciclopédico de Baja California.* Mexico City: Instituto de Cultura de Baja California.
Ascher, William. 1987. "Editorial: Policy Sciences and Economic Approach in the Post-Positivist Era," *Policy Sciences* 20:3–9.
Aziz Nassif, Alberto. 1987. "Electoral Practices and Democracy in Chihuahua, 1985." In *Electoral Patterns and Perspectives in Mexico,* edited by Arturo Alvarado Mendoza. Monograph Series, no. 22. La Jolla: Center for U.S.-Mexican Studies, University of California, San Diego.
Baer, M. Delal. 1990. "Electoral Trends." In *Prospects for Democracy in Mexico,* edited by George W. Grayson. New Brunswick, N.J.: Transaction Press.
Bailey, John J. 1988. *Governing Mexico: The Statecraft of Crisis Management.* New York: St. Martin's Press.
———. 1994. "Centralism and Political Change in Mexico: The Case of National Solidarity." In *Transforming State-Society Relations in Mexico: The National Solidarity Strategy,* edited by Wayne A. Cornelius, Ann L. Craig, and Jonathan Fox. U.S.-Mexico Contemporary Perspectives Series, no. 6. La Jolla, Calif.: Center for U.S.-Mexican Studies, University of California, San Diego.
Baja California. 1987. *Monografía del Estado de Baja California.* Mexicali, B.C.: Centro de Estudios Políticos, Económicos y Sociales, Partido Revolucionario Institucional.
———. 1989. *Informe de Gobierno de Baja California.* Mexicali, B.C.: Gobierno del Estado.
———. 1990. *Bases generales del Programa de Descentralización para el Fortalecimiento Municipal.* Mexicali, B.C.: Gobierno del Estado.
Barros Horcasitas, José Luis, Javier Hurtado, and Germán Pérez Fernández, eds. 1991. *Transición a la democracia y reforma del Estado en México.* Mexico City: Miguel A. Porrúa/FLACSO.
Bartra, Roger, et al. 1975. *Caciquismo y poder político en el México rural.* Mexico City: Siglo XXI.

Bath, C. Richard. 1989. "The Mexican Congress: A New Role." Presented at the annual meeting of the Rocky Mountain Council on Latin American Studies, University of New Mexico, Las Cruces.

Benson, Nettie Lee. 1958. "Spain's Contribution to Federalism in Mexico." In *Essays in Mexican History*, edited by Thomas Cotner and Carlos E. Castañeda. Austin: Institute of Latin American Studies, University of Texas at Austin.

Bezdek, Robert. 1995. "Democratic Changes in an Authoritarian System: *Navismo* and Opposition Development in San Luis Potosí." In *Opposition Government in Mexico*, edited by Victoria E. Rodríguez and Peter M. Ward. Albuquerque: University of New Mexico Press.

Bruhn, Kathleen, and Keith Yanner. 1995. "Governing under the Enemy: The PRD in Michoacán." In *Opposition Government in Mexico*, edited by Victoria E. Rodríguez and Peter M. Ward. Albuquerque: University of New Mexico Press.

Bustamante, Jorge A. 1985. "Surgimiento de la Colonia Libertad." In *Historia de Tijuana: semblanza general*, edited by David Pinera Ramírez. Tijuana, B.C.: Centro de Investigaciones Históricas, Universidad Nacional Autónoma de México/Universidad Autónoma de Baja California.

Camp, Roderic Ai. 1993. *Politics in Mexico*. New York: Oxford University Press.

———. 1995. "The PAN's Social Bases: Implications for Leadership." In *Opposition Government in Mexico*, edited by Victoria E. Rodríguez and Peter M. Ward. Albuquerque: University of New Mexico Press.

Carpizo, Jorge. 1978. *El presidencialismo mexicano*. Mexico City: Siglo XXI.

Carrillo V., Jorge. 1985. *Mujeres fronterizas en la industria maquiladora*. Tijuana, B.C.: Centro de Estudios Fronterizos del Norte de México.

CEE (Comisión Electoral Estatal). 1992. "Resultados Electorales Estatales y Municipales," *Boletín Estatal* (Gobierno del Estado de Baja California), August 31, p. 25.

Chávez Galindo, Ana María. 1987. *Migración, fecundidad y anticoncepción en Baja California: algunas hipótesis de trabajo*. Mexico City: Centro Regional de Investigaciones Multidisciplinarias, Universidad Nacional Autónoma de México.

Cockcroft, James D. 1983. *Mexico: Class Formation, Capital Accumulation, and the State*. New York: Monthly Review Press.

Colosio, Luis Donaldo. 1993. "Why the PRI Won the 1991 Elections." In *Political and Economic Liberalization in Mexico: At a Critical Juncture?* edited by Riordan Roett. Boulder, Colo.: Lynne Rienner.

CONAPO (Consejo Nacional de Población). 1988. *Demografía de la frontera norte de México*. Mexico City: CONAPO.

Connolly, P. 1993. "The Value of the Mexican Census for the Analysis of Housing and Infrastructure Issues in the Border Region." Presented at the Bi-National Census Symposium on the U.S.-Mexico Border, University of Texas at El Paso, March 29–31.

Contreras, Oscar F., and Vivienne Bennett. 1994. "National Solidarity in the Northern Borderlands: Social Participation and Community Leadership." In *Transforming State-Society Relations in Mexico: The National Solidarity Strategy*, edited by Wayne A. Cornelius, Ann L. Craig, and Jonathan Fox. U.S.-Mexico Contemporary Perspectives Series, no. 6. La Jolla: Center for U.S.-Mexican Studies, University of California, San Diego.

Cook, Maria Lorena. 1990. "Organizing Opposition in the Teachers' Movement in Oaxaca." In *Popular Movements and Political Change in Mexico*, edited by Joe Foweraker and Ann L. Craig. Boulder, Colo.: Lynne Rienner.

Cornelius, Wayne A. 1975. *Politics and the Migrant Poor in Mexico City*. Stanford, Calif.: Stanford University Press.

———. 1987. "Political Liberalization in an Authoritarian Regime: Mexico, 1976–85." In *Mexican Politics in Transition*, edited by Judith Gentleman. Boulder, Colo.: Westview.

———. 1994. "Mexico's Delayed Democratization," *Foreign Policy* 95 (Summer): 53–71.

Cornelius, Wayne A., and Ann L. Craig. 1991. *The Mexican Political System in Transition*. Monograph Series, no. 35. La Jolla: Center for U.S.-Mexican Studies, University of California, San Diego.

Cornelius, Wayne A., Ann L. Craig, and Jonathan Fox, eds. 1994. *Transforming State-Society Relations in Mexico: The National Solidarity Strategy*. U.S.-Mexico Contemporary Perspectives Series, no. 6. La Jolla: Center for U.S.-Mexican Studies, University of California, San Diego.

Cornelius, Wayne A., Judith Gentleman, and Peter H. Smith. 1989. "Overview: The Dynamics of Political Change in Mexico." In *Mexico's Alternative Political Futures*. Monograph Series, no. 30. La Jolla: Center for U.S.-Mexican Studies, University of California, San Diego.

Crespo, José Antonio. 1995. "Governments of the Opposition: The Official Response." In *Opposition Government in Mexico*, edited by Victoria E. Rodríguez and Peter M. Ward. Albuquerque: University of New Mexico Press.

Dahl, Robert Alan. 1956. *A Preface to Democratic Theory*. Chicago: University of Chicago Press.

de Gortari Rabiela, Hira. 1994. "El federalismo en la construcción de los estados." In *Mexico in the Age of Democratic Revolutions, 1750–1850*, edited by Jaime E. Rodríguez. Boulder, Colo.: Lynne Rienner.

Diesing, Paul. 1962. *Reason in Society: Five Types of Decisions and Their Social Conditions*. Chicago: University of Illinois Press.

Dresser, Denise. 1991. *Neopopulist Solutions to Neoliberal Problems: Mexico's National Solidarity Strategy*. Current Issue Briefs Series, no. 3. La Jolla: Center for U.S.-Mexican Studies, University of California, San Diego.

Fagen, Richard R., and William S. Tuohy. 1972. *Politics and Privilege in a Mexican City*. Stanford, Calif.: Stanford University Press.

Favela, Alejandro. 1992. "El gobierno salinista y la reforma del Estado," *Estudios Políticos* 3 (9): 55–73.

Foweraker, Joe. 1993. *Popular Mobilization in Mexico: The Teachers' Movement, 1977–87*. Cambridge: Cambridge University Press.

Foweraker, Joe, and Ann L. Craig, eds. 1990. *Popular Movements and Political Change in Mexico*. Boulder, Colo.: Lynne Rienner.

Fox, Jonathan, and Julio Moguel. 1995. "Pluralism and Anti-Poverty Policy: Mexico's National Solidarity Program and Left Opposition Municipal Governments." In *Opposition Government in Mexico*, edited by Victoria E. Rodríguez and Peter M. Ward. Albuquerque: University of New Mexico Press.

Garrido, Luis Javier. 1989. "The Crisis of *Presidencialismo*." In *Mexico's Alternative Political Futures*, edited by Wayne A. Cornelius, Judith Gentleman, and Peter

H. Smith. Monograph Series, no. 30. La Jolla: Center for U.S.-Mexican Studies, University of California, San Diego.
Gilbert, Alan, and Peter M. Ward. 1985. *Housing, the State and the Poor: Policy and Practice in Three Latin American Cities*. Cambridge: Cambridge University Press.
González Casanova, Pablo. 1970. *Democracy in Mexico*. New York: Oxford University Press.
González Oropeza, Manuel. 1983. *La intervención federal en la desaparición de poderes*. Mexico City: Instituto de Investigaciones Jurídicas, Universidad Nacional Autónoma de México.
Graham, Lawrence S. 1971. *Mexican State Government: A Prefectural System in Action*. Austin: Institute for Public Affairs, University of Texas at Austin.
———. 1993. "Rethinking the Relationship between the Strength of Local Institutions and the Consolidation of Democracy: The Case of Brazil," *In Depth* 3 (1): 177–193.
Guadarrama, Graciela S. 1987. "Entrepreneurs and Politics: Businessmen in Electoral Contests in Sonora and Nuevo León, July 1985." In *Electoral Patterns and Perspectives in Mexico*, edited by Arturo Alvarado Mendoza. Monograph Series, no. 22. La Jolla: Center for U.S.-Mexican Studies, University of California, San Diego.
Guillén López, Tonatiuh. 1992. "Baja California: una década de cambio político." In *Frontera norte: una década de política electoral*, edited by T. Guillén López. Tijuana, B.C.: El Colegio de la Frontera Norte.
———. 1993. *Baja California 1989–1992: alternancia política y transición democrática*. Tijuana, B.C.: El Colegio de la Frontera Norte/Centro de Investigaciones Interdisciplinarias en Humanidades, Universidad Nacional Autónoma de México.
Hansen, Roger D. 1974. *The Politics of Mexican Development*. 2d ed. Baltimore, Md.: Johns Hopkins University Press.
Harvey, Neil. 1989. "Personal Networks and Strategic Choices in the Formation of an Independent Peasant Organization: The OCEZ of Chiapas, Mexico," *Bulletin of Latin American Research* 7 (2): 299–312.
Hernández Rodríguez, Rogelio. 1991. "La reforma interna y los conflictos en el PRI," *Foro Internacional* 32 (2): 222–49.
Herzog, Lawrence A. 1990. *Where North Meets South: Cities, Space, and Politics on the U.S.-Mexico Border*. Austin: Center for Mexican American Studies, University of Texas at Austin.
Hiernaux, Daniel. 1986. *Urbanización y autoconstrucción de vivienda en Tijuana*. Mexico City: Centro de Ecodesarrollo.
Huntington, Samuel P. 1968. *Political Order in Changing Societies*. New Haven, Conn.: Yale University Press.
INEGI (Instituto Nacional de Estadística, Geografía e Informática). 1986. *Censo General de Población y Vivienda, 1980*. Mexico City: INEGI.
———. 1991. *Resultados oportunos de Baja California: censos económicos, 1989*. Aguascalientes, Ags.: INEGI.
Karl, Terry, and Philippe C. Schmitter. 1991. "Modes of Transition in Latin America, Southern and Eastern Europe," *International Social Science Journal* 128 (May): 269–284.

Klesner, Joseph. 1991. "Challenges for Mexico's Opposition in the Coming Sexenio." In *Sucesión Presidencial: The 1988 Mexican Presidential Election*, edited by Edgar W. Butler and Jorge A. Bustamante. Boulder, Colo.: Westview.

Krauze, Enrique. 1986. *Por una democracia sin adjetivos*. Mexico City: Joaquín Mortiz-Planeta.

Lorey, David E., ed. 1990. *United States-Mexico Border Statistics since 1990*. Los Angeles: UCLA Program on Mexico, University of California, Los Angeles.

Mabry, Donald J. 1974. "Mexico's Party Deputy System: The First Decade," *World Affairs* 16:2.

Madrazo, Jorge. 1985. "Reforma política y legislación electoral de las entidades federativas." In *Las elecciones en México: evolución y perspectivas*, edited by Pablo González Casanova. Mexico City: Siglo XXI.

Maxfield, Sylvia. 1990. *Governing Capital: International Finance and Mexican Politics*. Ithaca, N.Y.: Cornell University Press.

Medina, Luis. 1991. "Polls and Exit Polls in Mexican Elections." Presented at the Conference on Electoral Reform in Mexico, University of Texas at Austin, November 21–22.

Meyer, Lorenzo. 1989. "Democratization of the PRI: Mission Impossible?" In *Mexico's Alternative Political Futures*, edited by Wayne A. Cornelius, Judith Gentleman, and Peter H. Smith. Monograph Series, no. 30. La Jolla: Center for U.S.-Mexican Studies, University of California, San Diego.

———. 1993. "El presidencialismo: del populismo al neoliberalismo," *Revista Mexicana de Sociología* 2/93:57–82.

Middlebrook, Kevin J. 1986. "Political Liberalization in an Authoritarian Regime: The Case of Mexico." In *Elections and Democratization in Latin America, 1980–85*, edited by Paul W. Drake and Eduardo Silva. La Jolla: Center for Iberian and Latin American Studies, University of California, San Diego.

Middlebrook, Kevin J., ed. 1991. *Unions, Workers, and the State in Mexico*. U.S.-Mexico Contemporary Perspectives Series, no. 2. La Jolla: Center for U.S.-Mexican Studies, University of California, San Diego.

Mizrahi, Yemile. 1994. "Rebels without a Cause? The Politics of Entrepreneurs in Chihuahua," *Journal of Latin American Studies* 26 (1): 137–58.

Molinar Horcasitas, Juan. 1986. "The Mexican Electoral System: Continuity by Change." In *Elections and Democratization in Latin America, 1980–85*, edited by Paul W. Drake and Eduardo Silva. La Jolla: Center for Iberian and Latin American Studies, University of California, San Diego.

———. 1987. "The 1985 Federal Elections in Mexico: The Product of a System." In *Electoral Patterns and Perspectives in Mexico*, edited by Arturo Alvarado Mendoza. Monograph Series, no. 22. La Jolla: Center for U.S.-Mexican Studies, University of California, San Diego.

Molinar Horcasitas, Juan, and Jeffrey A. Weldon. 1994. "Electoral Determinants and Consequences of National Solidarity." In *Transforming State-Society Relations in Mexico: The National Solidarity Strategy*, edited by Wayne A. Cornelius, Ann L. Craig, and Jonathan Fox. U.S.-Mexico Contemporary Perspectives Series, no. 6. La Jolla: Center for U.S.-Mexican Studies, University of California, San Diego.

Musacchio, Humberto. 1989. *Diccionario Enciclopédico de México*. Mexico City: A. León.

Needler, Martin C. 1971. *Politics and Society in Mexico*. Albuquerque: University of New Mexico Press.
Nolasco, Margarita. 1989. *Los municipios de las fronteras de México*. Mexico City: Centro de Ecodesarrollo.
Ochoa Campos, Moisés. 1986. "La estructura del municipio mexicano," *Estudios Municipales* 10:133–66.
Ordóñez Barba, Gerardo. 1991. "Participación política y administración municipal: el caso de Ciudad Juárez (1980–89)." Master's thesis, El Colegio de la Frontera Norte, Ciudad Juárez.
Osborne, David. 1988. *Laboratories of Democracy*. Boston, Mass.: Harvard Business School Press.
PAN (Partido Acción Nacional). 1985. *Plataforma, 1985–1988*. Mexico City: PAN.
———. 1989. *Programa de Gobierno, 1989–1995*. Mexico City: PAN.
Pastor, Robert A. 1990. "Post-Revolutionary Mexico: The Salinas Opening," *Journal of InterAmerican Studies and World Affairs* 32 (3): 1–22.
Pick, James B., Edgar W. Butler, and Elizabeth L. Lanzer. 1987. *Atlas of Mexico*. Boulder, Colo.: Westview.
Price, John A. 1973. *Tijuana: Urbanization in a Border Culture*. Notre Dame, Ind.: University of Notre Dame Press.
Przeworski, Adam. 1986. "Some Problems in the Study of the Transition to Democracy." In *Transitions from Authoritarian Rule: Comparative Perspectives*, edited by Guillermo O'Donnell, Philippe C. Schmitter, and Laurence Whitehead. Baltimore, Md.: Johns Hopkins University Press.
Puertas Gómez, G. 1993. "Some Distinctive Traits of the Mexican Constitution: Description and Commentaries." Presented at the Houston Bar Association–Monterrey Business Lawyers Group, Houston, Tex., February.
Purcell, Susan K., and John Purcell. 1980. "State and Society in Mexico: Must a Stable Polity Be Institutionalized?" *World Politics* 32:194–227.
Ramírez Saiz, Juan Manuel. 1986. *El Movimiento Urbano Popular en México*. Mexico City: Siglo XXI.
Reding, Andrew. 1988. "The Democratic Current: A New Era in Mexican Politics," *World Policy Journal* 5 (2): 323–66.
Riva Palacio, Raymundo. 1993. "The Press and Politics in Mexico." Presented at the seminar "Mexico Anyone?" Mexican Center, Institute of Latin American Studies, University of Texas at Austin, April 6.
Rodríguez, Jaime E. 1994. "The Transition from Colony to Nation: New Spain, 1820–21." In *Mexico in the Age of Democratic Revolutions, 1750–1850*, edited by J. Rodríguez. Boulder, Colo.: Lynne Rienner.
Rodríguez, Victoria E. 1987. "The Politics of Decentralization in Mexico: Divergent Outcomes of Policy Implementation." Ph.D. dissertation, University of California, Berkeley.
———. 1992. "Mexico's Decentralization in the 1980s: Promises, Promises, Promises." In *Decentralization in Latin America: An Evaluation*, edited by Arthur Morris and Stella Lowder. New York: Praeger.
———. 1993. "Decentralization in Mexico: From Municipio Libre to Solidaridad," *Bulletin of Latin American Research* 12 (2): 133–45.
———. 1995. "Municipal Autonomy and the Politics of Intergovernmental Finance: Is It Different for the Opposition?" In *Opposition Government in*

Mexico, edited by V.E. Rodríguez and Peter M. Ward. Albuquerque: University of New Mexico Press.

———. n.d. *Decentralization in Mexico: The Facade of Power.* Boulder, Colo.: Westview. Forthcoming.

Rodríguez, Victoria E., and Peter M. Ward. 1992. *Policymaking, Politics, and Urban Governance in Chihuahua: The Experience of Recent PANista Governments.* Austin: U.S.-Mexican Policy Studies Program, Lyndon B. Johnson School of Public Affairs, University of Texas at Austin.

———. 1994a. "Disentangling the PRI from the Government in Mexico," *Mexican Studies/Estudios Mexicanos* 10 (1): 163–86.

———. 1994b. "From Machine Politics to the Politics of Technocracy: A Study in the Decline of Partisanship in Two Mexican Cities." Working Paper. Austin: Lyndon B. Johnson School of Public Affairs, University of Texas at Austin.

Rodríguez, Victoria E., and Peter M. Ward, eds. 1995. *Opposition Government in Mexico.* Albuquerque: University of New Mexico Press.

Rondinelli, Dennis A. 1990. *Decentralizing Urban Development Programs: A Framework for Analyzing Policy.* Washington, D.C.: U.S. Agency for International Development.

Rondinelli, Dennis A., and John R. Nellis. 1986. "Assessing Decentralization Policies in Developing Countries, Public and Private Roles in Urban Development: A Case for Cautious Optimism," *Development Policy Review* 4 (1): 3–23.

Salas-Porras Soulé, Alejandra, ed. 1989. *Nuestra frontera norte.* Mexico City: Editorial Nuestro Tiempo.

Schers, D. 1972. "The Popular Sector of the PRI in Mexico." Ph.D. dissertation, University of New Mexico.

Sherwood, F. 1969. "Devolution as a Problem of Organizational Strategy." In *Comparative Urban Research,* edited by Robert T. Daland. Beverly Hills, Calif.: Sage.

Simonowitz, Haskel. 1979. "Political Opposition in a Mexican Border State: The Partido Acción Nacional in Baja California Norte." Ph.D. dissertation, University of California, Riverside.

Sklair, Leslie. 1993. *Assembling for Development: The Maquila Industry in Mexico and the United States.* Rev. ed. U.S.-Mexico Contemporary Perspectives Series, no. 5. La Jolla: Center for U.S.-Mexican Studies, University of California, San Diego.

Smith, Peter H. 1979. *Labyrinths of Power: Political Recruitment in Twentieth-Century Mexico.* Princeton, N.J.: Princeton University Press.

Stephen, Lynn. 1991. *Zapotec Women.* Austin: University of Texas Press.

Valderrábano, Azucena. 1989. *Historias del poder: el caso de Baja California.* Mexico City: Grijalbo.

Valenzuela Arce, José Manuel. 1987. *El Movimiento Urbano Popular en Tijuana: reconstrucción testimonial.* Tijuana, B.C.: El Colegio de la Frontera Norte.

Vicencio, G. 1994. "The PAN's Administration in Baja California: The Struggle for a Free and Sovereign State." Presented at the Society of Latin American Studies meeting "Dismantling the Mexican State," Manchester, England, January 6–7.

Ward, Peter M. 1986. *Welfare Politics in Mexico: Papering over the Cracks.* Boston: Allen & Unwin.

———. 1993. "Social Welfare Policy and Political Opening in Mexico," *Journal of Latin American Studies* 25 (3): 613–28.

———. 1995. "Policy Making and Policy Implementation among Non-PRI Governments: The PAN in Ciudad Juárez and Chihuahua." In *Opposition Government in Mexico*, edited by Victoria E. Rodríguez and P.M. Ward. Albuquerque: University of New Mexico Press.

Ward, Peter M., et al. 1994. *Memoria of the Binational Conference: Mexico's Electoral Aftermath and Political Future*. Issues in Contemporary Mexico Working Paper Series. Austin: The Mexican Center, Institute of Latin American Studies, University of Texas at Austin.

About the Authors

VICTORIA E. RODRIGUEZ received her Ph.D. in Political Science in 1987 from the University of California, Berkeley. She is an Assistant Professor at the Lyndon B. Johnson School of Public Affairs, the University of Texas at Austin. Her current work includes a pathbreaking research project on women in contemporary Mexican politics. During the past four years she has codirected with Peter M. Ward a major research project on opposition governments in Mexico. In addition to the present work, they are coauthors of *Policymaking, Politics and Urban Governance in Chihuahua: The Experience of Recent Panista Governments* and coeditors of *Opposition Governments in Mexico*, which will be published in early 1995 by the University of New Mexico Press. She is the author of *Decentralization in Mexico: The Facade of Power* and of several articles and book chapters dealing with Mexican politics and public administration. Her principal research interests revolve around the broader topic of political and administrative decentralization in Mexico, particularly intergovernmental relations and municipal politics. In 1993–94 she served as a consultant for the World Bank on a project on decentralization and regional development in Mexico.

PETER M. WARD took his Ph.D. in Geography from the University of Liverpool in 1976 and held senior teaching positions at the Universities of London and Cambridge before moving to the University of Texas at Austin in 1991, where he is a Professor in the Department of Sociology and at the Lyndon B. Johnson School of Public Affairs. Since 1992 he has also been the Director of the Mexican Center of the Institute of Latin American Studies at UT. In addition to numerous articles and book chapters on public policy in Mexico and Latin America, his most recent books include *Housing, the State and the Poor: Policy and Practice in Latin American Cities* (coauthored with Alan Gilbert), *Welfare Politics in Mexico: Papering Over the Cracks*, and *Mexico City: The Production and Reproduction of an Urban Environment* (all translated into Spanish), *Corruption, Develop-*

ment and Inequality (editor), and *Methodology for Land and Housing Market Analysis* (coeditor). He is currently completing two major research projects: that of opposition government in Mexico (with Victoria Rodríguez) and a study on residential land values and land development policy in Mexico. His principal research interests are housing, planning, urban development, and the politics of public administration in Mexico. At various times he has served as adviser to the Mexican government and to several international development agencies.

CENTER FOR U.S.-MEXICAN STUDIES
UNIVERSITY OF CALIFORNIA, SAN DIEGO

Kevin J. Middlebrook, Acting Director

INTERNATIONAL ADVISORY COUNCIL

Víctor Espinoza del Valle
El Colegio de la Frontera Norte

Gary Gereffi
Duke University

Mercedes González de la Rocha
CIESAS–Occidente

Merilee S. Grindle
Harvard University

Joseph Grunwald
Graduate School of International
Relations and Pacific Studies, UCSD

Nora Lustig
Brookings Institution

Juan Molinar Horcasitas
El Colegio de México

Clemente Ruiz Durán
Universidad Nacional Autónoma
de México

Marcelo M. Suárez-Orozco
University of California, San Diego

Blanca Torres
El Colegio de México

Eric Van Young
University of California, San Diego

Laurence Whitehead
Oxford University

PUBLICATIONS PROGRAM
Kevin J. Middlebrook and Peter H. Smith, Codirectors
Sandra del Castillo, Managing Editor

Publication of important new research on Mexico and U.S.-Mexican relations is a major activity of the Center for U.S.-Mexican Studies. Statements of fact and opinion appearing in Center publications are the responsibility of the authors alone and do not imply endorsement by the Center for U.S.-Mexican Studies, the International Advisory Council, or the University of California.

For a complete list of Center publications and ordering information, please contact:

Publications Sales Office
Center for U.S.-Mexican Studies, 0510
University of California, San Diego
9500 Gilman Drive
La Jolla, CA 92093-0510

Phone: (619) 534-1160   FAX: (619) 534-6447
E-Mail: usmpubs@weber.ucsd.edu